SCHOOL'S OUT, LEARNING'S IN: HOME-LEARNING ACTIVITIES TO KEEP CHILDREN ENGAGED, CURIOUS, AND THOUGHTFUL

This book is an accessible guide to helping boost your child's language, curiosity, and problem-solving abilities outside of the classroom. Packed full of learning activities for children and teaching advice for parents, this book is specifically designed to support parents in engaging their children in thought-provoking conversations and problem-solving strategies.

Divided into two parts, the authors first guide readers through 'Learning Pit' theory, then present a range of lesson suggestions and useful resources for parents to draw on. This book will give you:

- ideas for learning with friends and family,
- tools to ensure your children make the most of the feedback,
- resource cards and practical suggestions with each activity, and
- confidence in your ability to impact your child's learning.

The perfect resource for parents supporting learning outside of school, *School's Out, Learning's In* will help you to boost your child's language, curiosity, and problem-solving abilities.

Jill Nottingham is Co-founder as well as Company Director of Challenging Learning. She is the principal author of the 200+ lesson resources they have online, as well as their two published lesson plan books. She is also a co-author of their books about feedback, dialogue, and early learning.

Carmen Bergmann is Senior Consultant and Regional Manager for Challenging Learning's work in North and South America. She has dedicated her adult life to improving education. She is especially passionate and involved in creating educational environments that are accessible and effective for all children.

James Nottingham is Co-founder of Challenging Learning and a leader in transforming up-to-date research into best practice for teaching and learning. He has also authored several books on encouraging learning and optimal classroom environments.

"At last! An accessible and invaluable resource for parents and carers. Nottingham and Bergmann guide you through the Learning Challenge principles, providing a great range of activities which will help your young people (and adults!)develop those key critical thinking skills. This book really will transform your conversations at the dinner table! Help your child to get into the Learning Pit and experience those 'eureka' moments."

—Lorna Pringle, English Teacher, Almouth, England

"An inspiring hands-on easy to use resource for all those parents/ teachers who want to develop children as lifelong learners both socially and academically."

—Deb Matley, Teacher, Ulladulla Public School, Australia

"At last – practical resources and lesson plans that will help parents engage in a rich learning experience with their children, whether learning at home or at school! This book shares the very best of how parents can support the learning journey, using the very best teaching and learning activities with choice and challenges built in along the way. This is a gift to all who want the very best for their children.

This book is what all parents need! It unlocks the mystery of what happens in a classroom and generously shares with it with parents in a way that is not only genuinely engaging but also reflective of the very best practice in education.

If I were to gift a book into the hands of parents about the learning of children, this would be it! This book unlocks the mysteries of the learning process by providing parents with activities and routines that are not only are the best ones that teachers use, but also in a way that will build relationship and understanding whether at home or at school.

This book will build the partnership between home and school beautifully. It is full of rich and engaging activities that are perfect for any part of the learning journey.

Parents (and teachers) have been waiting for a book like this for a long time! It generously shares the magic of the learning journey with all so that successful partnerships can be built between home and school. Parents will love dipping in and out of the rich resources - there is much to engage for many years!"

—Kate Cunich, Head of Academics and Innovation, Oxley College, NSW, Australia

"Do you want to practice your kids to get out of the comfort zone and allow them to think so that it creaks? (and allow them to think hard!) Do you want to give them the opportunity to doubt and practice listening and being curious about a statement other than their own?

If so, then this parenting edition is a really good book that is both easy and educational for you as a parent. You are supported, through the explanation of what "The Learning Pit" is and get a myriad of methods and ideas for how you can challenge your children's thinking.

The book gives you the opportunity to strengthen your children's imagination and philosophical thoughts when you around the dinner table, for example, talking about what joy is. For when do you know you are happy? How do you know that other people are happy? Do we all understand joy in the same way - and who decides what joy is?

12 different themes; you choose where you want to start - Being in The Pit strengthens your child's ability to be curious, determined and enduring.

And all children need to practice that. And adults too, for that matter."

—Lene Maagoee, District Manager, Glasaxe

"As both an educator and a parent, this book is an incredible resource for connecting parents and educators to encourage children's growth as learners. The resources in the text do not require fancy preparation. Instead, parents are given strategies and simple tools to further engage their children in the world around them and well beyond. Children have natural curiosity and with these concepts, parents can encourage those curiosities to develop children as critical thinkers, hard workers, and persistent thinkers. Most of all, their natural curiosities are encouraged and developed. I am more confident as a parent and an educator after reading and using this text. The organization of the text allows for meaningful engagement that is not staged or artificial. Rather, these concepts work at the dinner table, in the car, during quiet time, and playing outside.

The Three Little Pigs activities engaged our entire family for a period of several weeks. We read different versions of the tale, compared and contrasted, asked meaningful questions, and imagined our own versions. We have since replicated the activity with Little Red Riding Hood, Goldilocks and the Three Bears, and Hansel and Gretel."

—Molly Allen, Assistant Regional Superintendent, Illinois, USA

SCHOOL'S OUT, LEARNING'S IN: HOME-LEARNING ACTIVITIES TO KEEP CHILDREN ENGAGED, CURIOUS, AND THOUGHTFUL

Jill Nottingham, Carmen Bergmann, and James Nottingham

LONDON AND NEW YORK

First edition published 2022
by Routledge
2 Park Square, Milton Park, Abingdon, Oxon, OX14 4RN

and by Routledge
52 Vanderbilt Avenue, New York, NY 10017

Routledge is an imprint of the Taylor & Francis Group, an informa business

British Library Cataloguing-in-Publication Data
A catalogue record for this book is available from the British Library

Library of Congress Cataloging-in-Publication Data
Names: Nottingham, Jill, author. | Bergmann, Carmen, 1972- author. | Nottingham, James, author.
Title: School's out, learning's in : home-learning activities to keep children engaged, curious, and
    thoughtful / Jill Nottingham, Carmen Bergmann and James Nottingham.
Description: First edition. | Abingdon, Oxon ; New York, NY : Routledge, 2021.
Identifiers: LCCN 2021003685 (print) | LCCN 2021003686 (ebook) |
    ISBN 9780367772123 (hardback) | ISBN 9780367772130 (paperback) |
    ISBN 9781003170280 (ebook)
Subjects: LCSH: Learning. | Activity programs in education. | Problem solving in children. |
    Thought and thinking—Study and teaching (Elementary)
Classification: LCC LB1060 .N673 2021 (print) | LCC LB1060 (ebook) | DDC 370.15/23—dc23
LC record available at https://lccn.loc.gov/2021003685
LC ebook record available at https://lccn.loc.gov/2021003686

ISBN: 978-0-367-77212-3 (hbk)
ISBN: 978-0-367-77213-0 (pbk)
ISBN: 978-1-003-17028-0 (ebk)

Typeset in Swis
by Apex CoVantage, LLC

To Ava, Brianna, Harry, Lance, Peyton, and Phoebe.
You came along and thrust us into the Learning Pit.
You lead us down many a challenging path, inspire us to
question the world around us (as well as our sanity), and
teach us to be parents as well as the best educators we can be.
We are so very proud of you all.

CONTENTS

Chapter 4: Lessons about our world

Index   207

PREFACE

This book shares the best ways to support children through the Learning Pit®. As such, it will help to develop children's curiosity, determination, and perseverance.

We have divided the ideas into 12 themes, including choice, cost, heroes, happiness, language, risk, time, exploration, dreams, stealing, success, and conflict. The activities and recommended lines of questioning are designed to challenge, engage, inspire, and provoke dialogue so that your children understand important concepts in more depth.

The ideas are not designed to be followed verbatim; instead, we encourage you to look for the starting point most relevant to your children and then go from there. Pick the ideas that are most interesting or the ones that will cause them to think more. Don't go for the activities that are easy for them – unless you feel the need to give them a 'quick win'. Instead, select the activities that are *just beyond* their comfort zone and start from there.

The best teaching identifies where children are (in terms of knowledge, skills, and understanding) and then helps them to go beyond that. A pioneer of educational philosophy, Lev Vygotsky, called this the *zone of proximal development*. Today, most people would call it 'stepping out of your comfort zone'. The activities within this book are designed to do that – to take children out of their comfort zone and to cause them to think more, wonder more, ask questions, make connections, consider cause and effect, look for patterns, and so on.

To help structure your child's learning in such a way as to give them a sense of progress, we have built all our recommendations around a 'Learning Pit' journey (what we mean by this is described in more depth in Chapter 1). That 'journey' will enable your young learners to move from surface-level knowledge, through a state of 'wonder wobbling', to a 'eureka' moment in which they better understand the complexity and relevance of the concepts they have been thinking about.

The ideas build on our earlier work, including those published in British and international journals throughout the 1990s, and more recently in *Challenging Learning* (2010); *Challenging Learning Through Dialogue* (2017); *The Learning Challenge: Guiding Students Through the Learning Pit* (2017); *Learning Challenge Lessons – Primary* (2018); and *Learning Challenge Lessons – ELA* (2018).

Our main inspiration came originally from the tradition of Philosophy for Children (P4C), created by Matthew Lipman and Ann Margaret Sharpe. Indeed, Lipman's book *Thinking in Education* (Lipman, 2003) is one of the most well-thumbed books on our shelves. He, in turn, was influenced greatly by the educational philosopher John Dewey (1859–1952). Both of these men emphasised the need to develop the following personal habits, abilities, and attitudes:

1   An inquiring outlook coupled with an ability to articulate problems

2   A tendency to be intellectually proactive and persistent

3   A capacity for imaginative and adventurous thinking

4   A habit of exploring alternative possibilities

5   An ability to critically examine issues

6   A capacity for sound independent judgement

They also wrote about the following social habits and dispositions:

7   Actively listening to others and trying to understand their viewpoints

8   Giving reasons for what you say and expecting the same of others

9   Exploring disagreements reasonably

10 Being generally cooperative and constructive

11 Being socially communicative and inclusive

12 Taking other people's feelings and concerns into account

These 12 aims provide the perfect backdrop to this book. Each set of ideas and strategies we have written aim to build at least one of these abilities or attitudes.

With our very best wishes,

Jill Nottingham, Carmen Bergmann, and James Nottingham
September 2020

PART 1. THE LEARNING PIT

1. USING THE LEARNING PIT TO IGNITE LEARNING

1.0 THE LEARNING PIT INTRODUCTION

All of the activities in this book are based upon the Learning Pit. This model, created by James Nottingham in the early 2000s, illustrates the steps often encountered when learning something new (Figure 1.1). It describes the move from (1) knowing one or two things about a topic; to (2) knowing quite a lot about that topic but also unearthing some complexity or contradictory information; to (3) making sense of the information by sequencing, grouping, or in some way organising it; to (4) considering the journey taken and the lessons learned for future reference.

It also applies to learning a new skill or developing abilities, from (1) being able to perform a skill in a basic way, to (2) making some progress but also struggling with the complexity or application of the skill, to (3) developing some fluency or rhythm, to (4) feeling a sense of mastery and identifying the lessons learned along the way.

In many ways, the Learning Pit is a child-friendly representation of Vygotsky's (1978) zone of proximal development in that it describes the move from *current* ability to *potential* ability.

Vygotsky's theory includes the idea that if you do something you are already capable of, then you are in your comfort zone, whereas if you go beyond your current abilities and try something new – or try the same thing but in a different way – then you are in your *zone of proximal development*.

In other words, stick to what you know or are capable of currently, and you'll be practising; step out of your comfort zone and engage in something you haven't tried or thought about before and, more than likely, you'll be 'learning'.

The problem is, many children become anxious about stepping out of their comfort zone. They fear making mistakes or failing. Some worry that they will look foolish or stupid. Others have the sense that if they find something difficult then it proves they are just not that clever. Unwittingly, some parents make this situation worse by 'rescuing' their children from problems or even arranging things in such a way as to prevent any sense of struggle or failure.

That is not to say that parents shouldn't help their children, but it is to say that if parents are too quick to 'rescue' their offspring from struggle or disappointment, then they are likely reducing the benefits of learning. Indeed, we might even go as far as to say these parents 'steal' their

Figure 1.1 The Learning Pit in four stages

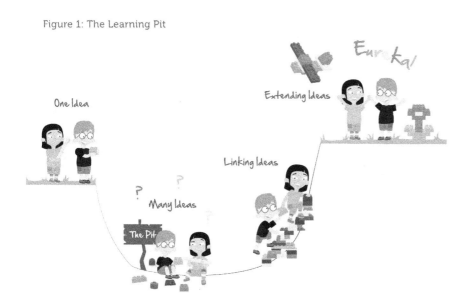

Figure 1: The Learning Pit

One Idea

Extending Ideas

Eureka!

Linking Ideas

Many Ideas

The Pit

children's success by completing the task for them. Think of the child who hasn't yet learned how to use a pair of scissors producing an amazing 3D model for homework, or the one whose writing is normally riddled with spelling mistakes returning a word-perfect piece of prose completed overnight. Can these 'successes' really be attributed to the children?

The Australians call overprotective parents *helicopter parents* – always hovering overhead to make sure their little darlings are doing okay. The Scandinavian equivalent is *curling parents*, from the winter Olympic sport of curling in which the competitors smooth the ice to help the stones slide further. The Japanese call them *bonsai parents*, changing the conditions to ensure their small 'trees' mimic the habits and appearance of mature, full-sized versions.

Helicopter parents monitor and guide their children's actions in the belief that this will help them to succeed. Unfortunately, this can be counterproductive. Analysis of multiple research studies show that children necessarily *have to* struggle if they are going to reap maximum reward from learning.

A British professor known for his extensive analysis of educational research studies and his transformation of feedback processes in schools wrote in 2016: 'If students do not have to work hard to make sense of what they are learning, then they are less likely to remember it in six weeks' time' (Dylan Wiliam, Emeritus Professor of Educational Assessment at UCL, London, 2016). Elizabeth and Robert Bjork, professors of psychology at the University of California in Los Angeles, offer similar conclusions from their research: 'When learners do well on a learning task, they are likely to forget things more quickly than if they do badly on the learning task; desirable difficulties enhance learning' (Bjork & Bjork, 2011). Bjork and Bjork go onto explain that 'learning' and 'performance' are distinctly different from each other and yet are often conflated to the point of giving false impressions of progress. If a child learns something with ease, they are likely to forget it with equivalent ease, whereas if their learning of a new skill or body of knowledge involves significant struggle, then they are likely to remember that learning long into the future. Furthermore, they are more likely to be able to apply that new skill or knowledge in other contexts rather than just in repeat situations. As the authors say, 'Conditions of learning that make performance improve rapidly often fail to support long-term retention and transfer, whereas conditions that create challenges and slow the rate of apparent learning often optimise long-term retention and transfer' (2011, p. 59). It seems therefore, that the old adage, 'easy come, easy go' is particularly relevant in learning theory.

This is why James Nottingham created the Learning Pit in the first place and why we have chosen to shape all our home-learning activities around the idea of making learning more challenging for children. We're not trying to be awkward or obstructive; instead, we're aiming to help children engage with 'desirable difficulties' so much that the benefits of their learning last long into the future.

1.1 COGNITIVE CONFLICT LEADS TO LONGER-LASTING LEARNING

Creating cognitive conflict in the minds of children is one way to encourage them to think more. Cognitive conflict – sometimes thought of as the educational equivalent of cognitive dissonance – is when a person holds two or more ideas that they agree with, but which are in conflict with each other. It is not about creating conflict *between* people but *within* people.

Everyday examples include the meat eater who believes killing animals for meat is cruel, the environmentalist who drives a gas-guzzling car, or the impulse buyers who say advertising doesn't work on them. The key to Learning Pit experiences is to deliberately create this sort of cognitive conflict in the minds of participants so that the result is more energetic, determined, and quizzical thinking and, ultimately, longer-lasting learning.

You might not want to talk about meat-eating or gas-guzzling, although of course you could if you thought it suitable for your children. Instead, you should select topics that are relevant and important to your children and then look for ways to create cognitive conflict in their minds. Or, as Bjork and Bjork call it, creating 'desirable difficulties to enhance learning'.

Examples of cognitive conflict that might be relevant to your children include the following:

    a   In maths, we're taught that odd numbers cannot be divided by two, but we all know that an odd number of friends could share a birthday cake between them.

b   We're told that stealing is wrong but that Robin Hood was right to steal from the rich and give to the poor.

c   Exercise is supposed to be good for us, but it also hurts when we do it sometimes and can lead to injury – neither of which feels good.

d   Love can't be measured, but love is also seen as a measure of how much we value something.

e   Telling the truth is encouraged, but sometimes lies are better.

f   We decide which is the best team by who wins the competition, but if a team cheats to win, then maybe they're not the best after all.

Examples from curriculum topics include the following:

g   In physics, there are *unstoppable forces* and *immovable objects*, but what if these two were to meet?

h   A single grain of millet makes no sound when falling, but a thousand grains make a sound; thus, a thousand 'nothings' become something.

i   Many people who value privacy and support legislation protecting people's privacy will post photographs and their own location information on social media.

j   Increasing the food available to an ecosystem may lead to instability, and even to extinction.

k   Applying pesticide to a pest may increase the pest's abundance.

l   Saturated fats are thought to be unhealthy, but the French diet is high in saturated fats, and yet they have low rates of heart disease.

m   A tragic hero deserves pity, but perhaps it is the victims who deserve pity, not the perpetrators.

n   Diluted nitric acid will corrode steel, but concentrated nitric acid will not.

Each of these examples ought to lead to head scratching. They should lead to someone thinking, 'on the one hand this is true, but on the other hand this is also true, and yet the two ideas contradict each other'.

In this state of cognitive conflict, you should witness children responding more thoughtfully and curiously. Whereas ordinarily, children who know the answer volunteer the information and children who don't keep quiet, in this situation, you should notice children who are more likely to suggest, wonder, connect, deliberate, and surmise. That is why all the activities in this book focus on creating cognitive conflict.

1.2 TAKING THE RIGHT APPROACH TO COGNITIVE CONFLICT

As you read through this book, you will notice that each activity is predicated on the intention to create – or respond constructively to – cognitive conflict, not so as to permanently confuse your children but so as to prompt them to think more, wonder more, look for ways to solve problems, think about meanings and implications, and so on.

It is important to approach this cognitive conflict with the right attitudes. These include:

1.2.1 Playfulness, not point scoring

Have fun with the activities in this book. Play with the ideas. Use phrases such as 'I'm confused', 'this is confusing me', 'I wonder what would happen if . . . ', and so on. Go into the Learning Pit with your children.

When your children were toddlers, you imitated drinking from a plastic tea set, feigned illness so that they could put on their medical outfits to cure you, and you probably pretended to cry when they pushed you away or did something you wanted to discourage. Not once did you say 'no, that's not right – you can't cure someone with a toy thermometer'! So it is with the activities in this book; don't say 'no, that's not right'. Instead, play along with them by asking questions such as 'that's an interesting idea, why do you say that?' or 'do you think it always works that way?' and so on. Indeed, we've included some questioning phrases and techniques you might like to use later in this book.

1.2.2 Be open-minded

Try not to give the impression that there is a 'right answer', even if you think there is. Of course, there could be occasions when your children say something that goes against your values, in which case you might feel obliged to correct them. But, in so far as possible, tread gently and try not to dissuade or chastise your children for any of the ideas they explore during these activities. Instead, ask questions about reasons, implications, connections, and examples so that they are prompted to think more and seek out the best ideas for themselves.

If, for example, your child suggests bullying a bully is the right thing to do, or taking revenge is permissible, then avoid responding with, 'two wrongs don't make a right'. Instead, ask questions such as 'what is bullying?' or 'how do we know if someone is a bully?' or 'is revenge the same as justice?'

Our purpose in recommending this approach is not to start on the slippery slope towards moral relativism in which anything is permissible so long as you can justify it. Rather, it is to suggest that children will become more reasonable when they learn to reason, more thoughtful when they learn to think for themselves, and more empathetic when they engage in dialogue with others. So instead of correcting children, which tends to close down any conversation, we would be better off listening carefully and responding with exploratory questions so that children learn how to think for themselves.

1.2.3 Challenge is interesting

Often, children (and indeed adults) view challenge as something 'difficult', whereas if we talk about challenges as being 'interesting' or 'intriguing', then children are less likely to be disheartened or fearful of stepping out of their comfort zone. Indeed, there is worrying evidence in educational research showing that when students are given choices in school, they all too often pick the easier option because of a worry that the alternatives are difficult. However, if we describe those very same alternatives as 'interesting' rather than difficult, the research indicates that children are more likely to have a go at them, which in turn is more likely to lead to enhanced learning outcomes.

1.2.4 Use dialogue to enhance learning

Dialogue that is open, engaging, and exploratory will teach your children so many good habits of thinking that it begs the question, why aren't most educational experiences based upon high-quality dialogue? Indeed, dialogue has been shown time and again to improve learning and yet is all too often dominated by adults. Gad Yair (2000) found that in schools, teachers talk for 70–80 per cent of the lesson time. The situation is even worse when teaching older students or fewer students. Indeed, a teacher working with 15 teenagers is much more likely to dominate the conversation than a teacher working with 30 seven-year-olds! In the home, this percentage will vary wildly depending on personalities, opportunities, and expectations.

Back in the '80s, Mary Budd Rowe (1986) found that when dialogue is placed at the heart of learning, significant gains can be made by all learners. One of her proposals was to ask adults to wait a minimum of three seconds after asking a question before saying anything else. The main purpose of this was to give children more time to think and respond, and yet Rowe also found that

- the length of answers or explanations given by children in response to teacher questions increased fivefold (sevenfold for children from disadvantaged backgrounds);
- the number of appropriate answers volunteered by students significantly increased;
- failures to respond or phrases such as 'I don't know' decreased from 30 per cent to less than 5 per cent;
- the number of questions asked by children increased significantly;
- scores on national and regional tests increased.

So, the lesson from that research is clear: don't be afraid of silence! Or put another way, stop talking so much and let your children do some thinking aloud.

1.3 QUESTIONING TECHNIQUES TO ENGAGE CHILDREN

One of the best ways to create cognitive conflict – and to encourage children to think more – is through the use of questioning – not questioning as if to interrogate, but rather to inquire, wonder together, and prompt further thought.

The following questioning techniques will help with this.

Clarification

a   Are you saying that . . . ?

b   What does that mean?

c   Could you rephrase that?

d   Could you explain that a little more?

e   Could someone else say what they think this idea means?

Reasons

f   Why do you think that?

g   What evidence/proof do you have for saying . . . ?

h   Could you give us an example?

i   Could someone else give an example or counterexample?

j   Do your reasons support your conclusion?

Assumptions

k   What do we already know about this?

l   Are you assuming that . . . ?

m   What are we taking for granted?

n   Are you suggesting that . . . ?

o   How could we be sure of this?

Viewpoints

p   What would happen if . . . ?

q   Who or what would benefit from this?

r   Who or what would be disadvantaged by . . . ?

s   Are there alternative ways of looking at this?

t   When would it be better/worse/different?

Equivalence

u   Are there similarities between this and that?

v   What are the main differences between this idea and that one?

w   Is this the same idea as before but put in a different way?

x   Are these ideas of equal value?

y   How would you rank these ideas from most to least . . . ?

Review

z   Which question led to the most progress, thought, confusion, etc.?

When using any of these questioning techniques, the aim should be to

1   challenge ideas, reasons, and assumptions;

2   make learners **wobble**;

3   lead to deeper thinking;

4   encourage learners to construct new meaning with deeper understanding.

1.4 THE LANGUAGE OF THE LEARNING PIT

As you begin using the activities in this book, you will notice frequent reference to the Learning Pit and its associated language. The main terms you will come across will be as follows.

Concept: a general idea that groups things together according to common characteristics. Activities that are designed to take children through the Learning Pit typically tend to focus on at least one key concept.

Concept stretching: a way to describe the actions involved in challenging learners' notions and applications of different concepts. For example, if your children thought a 'hero' was someone who takes risks, then you could 'stretch' their ideas by questioning if someone could take risks without being a hero (e.g., risking their life by playing games on a railway line) or if someone could be a hero without taking risks (e.g., some people would say a relative of theirs is their 'hero', not because they take risks but because of other qualities they personify).

Construct: the process of creating understanding by going beyond first ideas or answers; seeking alternative explanations; asking questions such as why, if, and what about; making connections; and finding the significance of parts in relation to the whole. It is this construction of new meanings and connections that leads children out of the Learning Pit.

Eureka: the sense of discovery a learner feels when they have a breakthrough after having struggled to understand or accomplish something. This sense of elation galvanises many children into wanting to find other challenges to overcome, which in itself is a positive sign that the Learning Pit is working.

Scaffolds: a collective term for a variety of strategies and tools used to help children move from a sense of panic or defeat to one in which, though still struggling, they feel a sense of direction and progress. For example, we might encourage children to use a Venn diagram to help them sort and classify their ideas so that they move from being overwhelmed to feeling organised. In this sense, the Venn diagram is a scaffolder.

Social constructivism: the theory that learning is an active process in which knowledge and understanding are constructed through social interaction with others. The emphasis is on 'constructed with' rather than 'acquired from' others. In this sense, a child learns more from constructing a definition as they go through the Learning Pit than they would from being given the same definition by an adult.

Understanding: the mental process of a person who comprehends. It includes an ability to explain cause, effect, and significance and to understand patterns and how they relate to each other – all of which are likely outcomes of a journey through the Learning Pit.

Wobbling, wobblers, and **being in the pit:** terms to describe a state of cognitive conflict in which a person holds two or more ideas that are seemingly agreeable while also being contradictory (for example, children shouldn't talk to strangers but they should also be polite by greeting people they don't know).

1.5 THE FOUR STAGES OF THE LEARNING PIT

The Learning Pit framework has four stages:

CONCEPT – choosing a key concept that your children are familiar with. This concept will form the basis for questioning and 'concept stretching'.

CONFLICT – creating cognitive conflict in your children's mind in order to take them into the Learning Pit. This sense of conflict between two or more ideas should lead to deeper and more productive thinking.

CONSTRUCT – constructing meaning by connecting, analysing, sorting, categorising, and grouping ideas into an arrangement that is accurate and makes sense to your children.

CONSIDER – inviting children to consider their journey through the Learning Pit, to think about the ways in which their thinking has changed, and to identify the strategies they used that could be applied in other contexts.

1.6 STAGE 1: CONCEPT

Someone could be in the Learning Pit whenever they have some basic knowledge and/or skill that they are struggling to apply in particular ways. It is *not* when they have *no* idea or skill, but rather when they have *at least* two or more ideas or ways of doing things that make sense to them despite those ideas conflicting with each other – for example, 'it would be easier to switch back to my dominant foot because kicking with my weaker foot is too hard and makes me look like I can't play very well; but, on the other hand, I know I will be a better player if I learn how to kick equally well with either foot'.

In this book, Learning Pit experiences focus on concepts. Generally speaking, we have selected abstract concepts because these lend themselves very well to dialogue and cognitive conflict. That does not mean more 'concrete' concepts can't be used; for example, you could create cognitive conflict around a concept as seemingly concrete as a 'table' – it has four legs (but so does a chair); food is placed on it at mealtimes (but you could use your lap for the same purpose); it has a flat surface to place things on (but so does a countertop or a sideboard); it is different from a chair because you wouldn't normally sit on a table (but of course, you *could* sit on a table); and so on.

As you peruse the activities we have designed, look for the concepts you think your children will be familiar with. They don't need to be able to talk at length about the concept, but they should at least be familiar with it. For example, if you plan to take a five-year-old into the Learning Pit, then the concept 'gravity' is unlikely to mean enough to them to be able to create cognitive conflict in their minds, whereas asking that same child what an 'animal' is or whether a teddy bear can be a 'pet' is much more likely to start things off well.

1.7 STAGE 2: CONFLICT

Stage two of the Learning Pit is concerned with creating cognitive conflict. We have created a wide range of methods to achieve this, including the following.

1.7.1 Dinner table conversations

These questioning sequences are designed to provide the groundwork for you and your child to explore the concepts which are highlighted by each set of activities. It may be helpful to start with at least one of them before diving into the activities to establish basic understanding and make initial connections. The rest can take place throughout the time that you are engaged with the lessons.

These sequences, and the ones included with the activities, are not meant to be a script, but rather a guide to help you and your child get started with this type of exploratory dialogue. Feel free to add in your own questions or change them to suit your own context. Hopefully, the more you engage in dialogue with questions like these, the more you and your child will naturally come up with your own questions.

Remember that, in order to build new meaning and extend learning, we want to create opportunities for Wonder Wobbles. Feeling some frustration about questioning our current thinking is a good thing. Be careful about providing answers, rather just keep asking more questions. The goal is not to arrive at definitive answers; it is to extend meaning and explore new ideas. These skills of learning will help your child to unpack new knowledge and achieve a deeper level of understanding.

1.7.2 Literacy connections

Literature is a great way to encourage the exploration of new and existing ideas. We have included connections to a variety of texts and stories throughout the activity sets. Many of these stories can be accessed online as read-aloud videos. Many schools and libraries are also likely to have copies that may be borrowed.

The books and stories referenced are, of course, merely suggestions. You can explore the concepts using many different stories. You can easily adapt the ideas and questions to fit the books and stories that you have access to. The key with these activities is to provide a context and setting around which you and your child can have dialogue about the concept. It may be easier for your child to thoroughly explore and consider new ideas when they are tied to fictional characters rather than themselves.

While putting our ideas in writing is difficult for some, it is a very good way to secure and preserve our thoughts. The process of writing requires us to clarify our ideas as we choose the words that best express our thinking. It also allows us to see growth and change in our thinking by coming back to our writing after time has passed. For these reasons, we have included a variety of writing activities. Even if your child is too young to do the writing themselves, it can be extremely valuable to engage in the suggested activities. Let your child tell you their stories or poems while you transcribe. This has the added value of helping your child to see the direct connection between verbal dialogue and writing, making the writing process feel more natural for them.

1.7.3 Maths connections

A study conducted in 2007 (Moser et al., 2011) looked at the brain activity that occurs when students are engaged with maths work. They found more brain activity and connections occurring when students made mistakes than when they were correct. It is this activity and resulting connections in the brain that allow for growth. We want to engage students in mathematical problems that challenge them and cause them to look at the maths in multiple ways so that they can grow in their skills and thinking.

We have included maths activities that allow for many different ability levels to access them. It is good for children to explore new concepts in mathematics without being told exactly what to do with them, and it is imperative that they be allowed to make mistakes so that they can create more connections and develop a deeper understanding of what does not work and why.

While it may feel uncomfortable, let your child struggle with the maths concepts that are introduced, and resist the temptation to provide them with step-by-step solutions. Use the questioning sequences to help them explore and wonder, and reassure them that it is okay to not understand everything just yet. You will be helping to develop a maths confidence that will benefit your child in the long run.

1.7.4 STEM connections

Many of the activity sets include the integration of science, technology, engineering, mathematics, and art skills and thinking. This integration will help children to see common patterns and systems that exist in our world and how they connect to the concepts being studied. You can enhance this learning by using questioning and dialogue to help your child identify these common patterns and systems, not just within each concept, but also between concepts.

As you look for additional activities to use with your child, look for opportunities where they are creating and designing models to solve problems or understand a concept. This could mean drawing pictures to solve maths problems, designing structures to test and understand concepts like gravity and movement, drawing pictures to express ideas, etc. This way of exploring will help your child to develop a deeper understanding of the concepts.

1.7.5 Games

Game play is an excellent way to engage even the most reluctant learners. It is in our nature to enjoy the competition and human interaction that occurs when playing games. Not only is it a great way to practice skills, it is also an opportunity to explore ideas through entertaining dialogue. When playing games, we enhance our ability to think strategically and flexibly as we plan our moves and actions based on what is happening in the game. The best way to build on the skills that are developed through game play is to talk about it and share our thinking.

We have added questioning sequences to extend the benefits of the game play. Enjoy playing the games and adding your own twists and rules, but don't forget to ask questions as you explore the strategies you and your child are using while playing. Talk about what guides your moves and actions and what you are thinking about doing next.

While it may be tempting to let your child win every game and to save them from making moves that are not strategic, these actions may have a negative impact on their growth mindset. Game play can also be used to help your child develop their growth mindset if they are able to experience improvement and growth. When you talk about and share strategies while playing the game, your child has the opportunity to apply them in subsequent games. If they struggle to win games at first, they may feel some frustration, but this will turn to excitement when they are able to apply learned strategies that result in wins later on.

1.8 STAGE 3: CONSTRUCT

Stage three of the Learning Pit begins when children start to clarify, connect, and sort the ideas they've been confused about. It is when the 'fog' begins to lift, and possible solutions present themselves. This sometimes takes place in an impromptu manner, whereas at other times, it requires the help of one of the 'pit tools' described on the following pages. Almost always, the timing of children's ascent 'out of the pit' varies dramatically from child to child and context to context. This variability is not something to worry about, but it is something to be aware of.

It is interesting to note that many people worry about this stage. Indeed, whenever we share the Learning Pit with teachers or parents, somebody always asks, 'What happens if I get them into the pit but can't get them out again?'

Our response to this is as follows:

1   When children are in the pit, they will naturally look for ways to come out again by making sense of their conflicting thoughts and finding solutions to their conundrum. So, often, all the adult will need to do is help children identify and apply the best sense-making strategy at the right time; the child's desire for clarity will do the rest.

2   The purpose of the Learning Pit is to think more, question more, and engage more. This means a 'quick exit' from the state of cognitive conflict is not necessarily a good thing. Often times, it is better to do what you can to keep children in the pit longer. A technique that fits nicely with this idea is to pair a child who has come out of the pit with one who has yet to do so and then to give instructions along these lines:

    The person who is out of the pit should try to help their partner who is still in the pit to come out. However, it is the responsibility of the person still in the pit to try to pull theirs partner back into the pit! Do not let them get away with easy answers! Question them; challenge them; ask 'what if' and 'what about' questions. Make sure they haven't just jumped out of the pit by sheer luck. We need to make sure everyone has developed a rock-solid understanding of the concept we're thinking about.

3   Sometimes, it is advantageous to leave children in the pit – depending on context and purpose. For example, if children are considering 'what is fair' then it might be preferable for them to struggle with their ideas for many days so that they can explore the concept in a variety of circumstances. In contrast, we might be more inclined towards helping them out of the pit if, for example, they are struggling to understand why an odd number is defined as 'not being divisible by two' when it's clear to them that two people *could* share an odd number of cakes. Helping them out of the pit would be particularly important if you are planning for children to apply their new understanding almost immediately.

On this last point, it would be worth saying that a lot of knowledge is based on sets of clearly defined answers that children need to know and apply. The side effect of this is that some children might then suppose that *every* question has an agreed-upon and clearly defined answer.

However, what are the 'agreed and defined' answers to questions such as 'is genetic modification a good thing?'; 'who was to blame for the deaths of Romeo and Juliet?'; 'what makes a true hero?'; 'should all laws be obeyed?'; 'where does matter come from?'; 'are exams easier or harder than 50 years ago?'; 'what makes us human?'; 'should family *always* come first?'; 'what is the right response to climate change?'; and so on? These questions and many more besides are unanswerable, at least in an absolute sense, so perhaps giving children the opportunity to experience situations in which they can't fully answer a question is an important preparation for the bigger questions in life.

The following section describes some of the Learning Pit tools. Each of them can be used to construct meaning and assist children in climbing out of the pit.

1.8.1 Concept target

A concept target can help your child make connections between vocabulary words and concepts or themes. By questioning the relative association of the word to the concept it builds deeper understanding of the general idea.

To use a concept target, your child should draw an inner and outer circle as shown in Figure 1.2. In the inner circle, they should write the key concept or theme; in the outer circle, they should write all the ideas and vocabulary that relate to that concept or that have emerged through the dialogue process.

Your child should take each idea in turn and decide whether it is a necessary characteristic of the concept (in which case they should move it to the inner circle), a probable characteristic (in which case they should leave it in the outer circle), or a very rare characteristic (in which case they should move it outside of the outer circle).

Figure 1.2 Concept targets

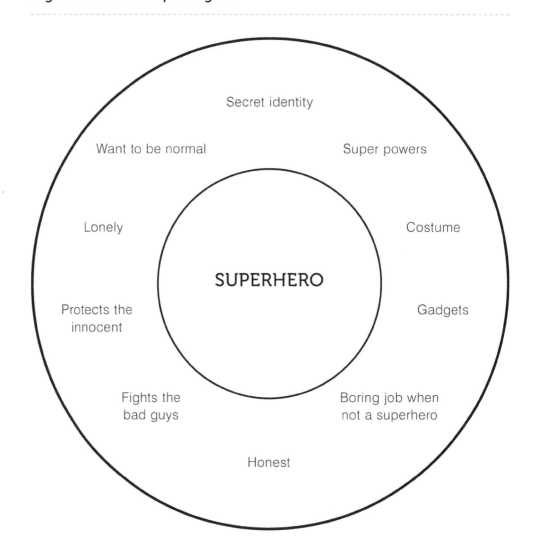

Figure 1.2 (Continued)

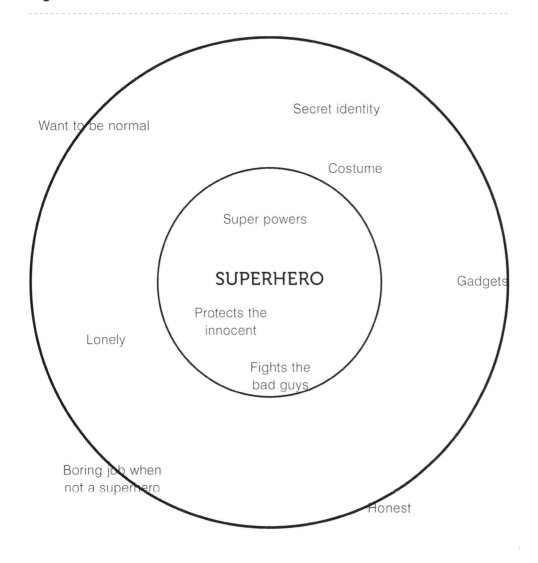

1.8.2 Ranking

A useful way for your child to sort through all their ideas is through ranking. This can be done in a linear ranking, a diamond ranking, a pyramid ranking, or any such shape that will prompt your child to analyse the relative value of each answer. Each time we have suggested ranking in the learning activities, we have given our recommendation as to the style to go for. Do not feel obliged to stick to this type of ranking; if another shape seems more appropriate, then encourage your child to go for that instead.

Please note that some children will be tempted to simply 'rank' characteristics in alphabetical order, particularly when they are finding the idea of ranking too challenging. If your child does this, then gently remind them that the task is not to 'sort' but to 'rank' and that alphabetical order is not a rank. If alphabetical order was indeed a rank, then words beginning with A would be seen as more valuable than words beginning with B, C, or D!

1.8.3 Diamond ranking

The diamond ranking strategy encourages active participation. It will help your child to prioritise information, clarify their thoughts, and create reasons and reflections.

Your child must place the statement or word with the highest priority at the top of the formation and the least important statement at the bottom. The second, third, and fourth rows consist of statements that are ranked with descending priority, with each row having two, three, and two statements, respectively. The diamond ranking looks like the illustration shown in Figure 1.3.

Figure 1.3 Diamond ranking

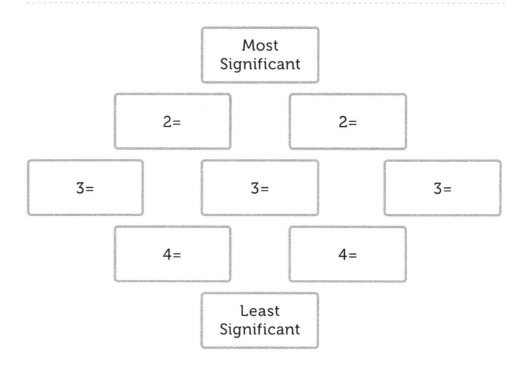

1.8.4 Pyramid ranking

A pyramid ranking (Figure 1.4) is similar to a diamond ranking except that it is in the shape of a pyramid or triangle. This allows different numbers of factors to be ranked compared to a diamond ranking.

Figure 1.4 Pyramid ranking

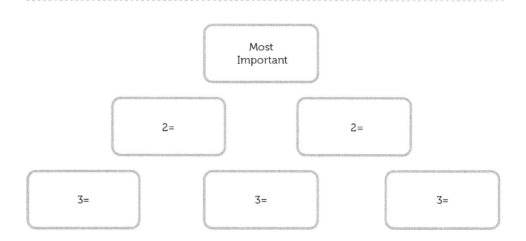

1.8.5 Linear ranking

A linear ranking (Figure 1.5) often leads to more deliberation than the other two styles of ranking because there are no 'equal' spots. Instead, each characteristic should be given a position that is different from any other. As with all the other ranks, though, this position can be decided on importance, relevance, significance, or any other agreed-upon quality.

Challenging LEARNING | The Learning Pit

Figure 1.5 Linear ranking

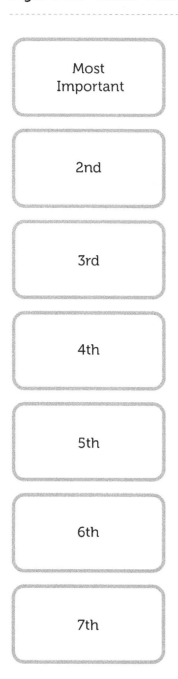

1.8.6 Odd one out

Your child is presented with a group of objects, numbers, words, text passages, poems, shapes, etc. to be compared and contrasted. They are then asked to identify the odd one out. This apparently simple question encourages your child to explore and focus on the characteristics of the items in question and to foster an understanding of relationships between them. There should be a large number of possible correct answers, and your child should always be encouraged to provide a fully explained and justified answer. The activities in this book use groups of three images, and this is the recommended number for making odd one out work successfully.

Asking your child to make *each* item or image the odd one out will encourage them to go beyond their first idea and to explore further possibilities. This can serve to deepen their thinking. Collecting and recording your child's thinking on a piece of paper is a good idea because this helps to make their thinking visible for them. This task works well to consolidate and extend their understanding of related vocabulary.

In odd one out, you look at three objects or pictures and discuss which one does not belong with the other two and why. Odd one out helps to build sorting, classifying, and reasoning language. Make it a challenge to find as many reasons as possible to make each object or picture the odd one out and always ask for details. Pick random objects without a 'right answer'. Keep asking questions and trying to find as many reasons as possible to make each item the odd one out.

1.8.7 Opinion lines

Opinion lines (Figure 1.6) are very useful for beginning to explore statements using examples, gauging degrees of agreement and disagreement, or identifying degrees of preference.

Figure 1.6 Opinion line from 'strongly agree' to 'strongly disagree'

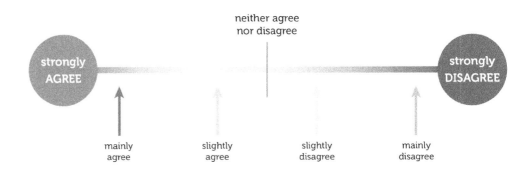

Using an opinion line

1   Create a line long enough to place statements along. This can be done as a horizontal line across a large sheet of paper or a physical line made with rope or string on the tabletop or floor.

2   Mark one end as 'strongly agree' and the other as 'strongly disagree'. Talk through the other descriptors shown in this diagram if you think it will help your child to understand the degrees of agreement and disagreement.

3   Share the statements with your child and give them time to think about each one in turn, placing it on the line depending on how much they agree or disagree with it.

4   The following question stems can be used to encourage dialogue:

   •   Why do you feel that way?

   •   What do you mean by . . . [choose a word from their answer]?

   •   What assumptions are you making in saying that you disagree?

   •   How could you change the statement/question so that you would move it to the other end of the line?

   •   What made you choose 'mostly agree' and 'not agree'? Or 'mostly disagree' and 'not disagree'?

1.8.8 Concept lines

Concept lines (Figure 1.7) have a similar structure to opinion lines and so can be used in a similar way. The main difference is that the line now represents characteristics of a concept rather than degrees of agreement or disagreement.

Encourage your child to list all terms and ideas that they have used in connection with the central concept. Then get them to place the terms along the line, being careful to place them in order of meaning or significance.

Figure 1.7 Concept line

Concept: Friendliness

Fanatical   Devoted   Forthcoming   Loyal   Dependable   Welcoming   Responsive   Approachable   Unsociable   Reserved   Disloyal   Distant   Hostile

This also works if you choose two extremes – for example, 'fair' and 'unfair' – write each word on a piece of paper, and place the two pages two to three metres apart. Choose ten games from around the house and place them in order between the extremes. Use the following question stems to increase dialogue:

- How is this game more/less fair than this game?
- What makes this game the fairest?
- How could you make this game fairer?
- How do you decide if a game is fair?
- What does it mean to be fair?
- If there are no winners and losers, could a game be unfair?
- If you always win a game, can it be fair?

1.8.9 Scavenger hunts

Scavenger hunts can be used as you explore concepts as a way to get your child thinking on their own about the concept. They do not require any preparation and can be used when you are just starting to explore a concept or after you have already spent time exploring a concept. For example, if you are talking about numbers, you can send your child off to find ten items that have numbers. Once they find the items, don't forget to deepen their learning by asking questions and engaging in dialogue about them. You can follow up with questions like these:

- How are numbers used differently on these items?
- Do numbers always represent a quantity? What else to they represent?
- Can you think of other items in the house that may use numbers in a different way?
- If a number is spelled out, is it still a number?

You can also use scavenger hunts to explore more abstract concepts, like 'useful'. Have your child find ten items that are useful. Follow up with questions like these:

- Why did you choose this item?
- Is this item always useful? Do you have any items that are only useful part of the year?
- Would this be useful to everyone?

1.8.10 Sorting and classifying with Venn diagrams

Sorting and classifying are everyday, often unconscious, skills that we use to organise information and ideas.

These are basic cognitive skills needed by all human beings to recognise similarities and differences through seeing common features, developing awareness of concepts, and making links between them. Sorting and classifying helps children to make sense of the world around them.

Venn diagrams are great visual tools for thinking and effectively support the process of sorting and classifying. They even work with the youngest children so long as you separate out the overlapping category into a third circle (Figure 1.8a).

Figure 1.8a

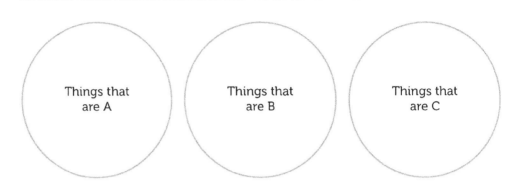

Of course, the normal way to draw a Venn diagram is as shown in Figure 1.8b with the overlapping circles.

Figure 1.8b

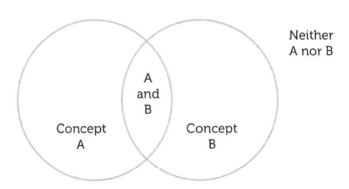

You can draw circles on paper, cut out circles of card, use string or rope to form circles or use rings to set up this activity. Your child should then sort the words or pictures into the appropriate set or circle. For example, if one circle is labelled 'pets' and the other is labelled 'wild animals', then they would place the puppy in the 'pet' circle and the tiger in the 'wild animal' circle. If they notice some that could be a wild animal AND a pet, set them aside and then talk about the need for a third category – animals that can be pets AND wild. You can use three separate rings, or you can overlap them to create the common space (Figure 1.8c).

Figure 1.8c

1.8.11 Opinion corners

Opinion corners (Figure 1.9) have a similar structure to opinion lines, so they can be used in a very similar way. The main difference is that using the corners will prevent your child from sitting on the fence because corners require them to choose from one of four descriptors: (1) strongly agree, (2) agree, (3) disagree, and (4) strongly disagree.

Figure 1.9

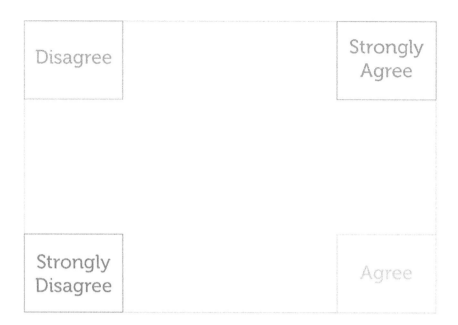

Mark out the four corners on a large piece of paper or using a space on the floor. Read through the statements with your child and discuss each one. Your child should decide which corner they feel that statement should be placed in according to how much they disagree with it or not. They cannot place a statement in the middle. They are allowed to move the statement if they change their mind after further thought and questioning, but it always needs to be placed in one of the four corners.

1.8.12 Mystery

A Mystery is a problem-solving activity based around a central question that is open to more than one reasonable answer.

The information or 'clues' needed to answer the question are presented on separate slips of paper or cards so that your child can analyse, sort, sequence, and link them together.

The questions at the heart of mysteries tend to be matters of interpretation, judgement, and argument. They often involve dialogues on causation or speculation about consequences.

Characteristics of a Mystery include the following:

1. They begin with a key question or dilemma that should create cognitive conflict in the mind of your child.
2. They generally revolve around a central character.
3. Some clues include ambiguous information.
4. Some clues include irrelevant or contradictory information.
5. Some clues are pure red herrings designed to deter easy answers.
6. Some clues can't be fully understood in the absence of other clues.
7. The subject matter ought to be relevant and of interest to participants.

1.8.13 Using a Mystery

Print out the clue cards, cut them up, and mix them up. Working at a table or on the floor, spread the clues out with your child and begin to read and sort through the information on them. They should use the information and their thinking skills to construct an answer to the key question that they can back up or justify with reasoning and evidence from the clue cards.

The following are some of the thinking and dialogue skills you should encourage your child to use:

Sorting relevant information

Checking and refining

Interpreting information

Explaining, reasoning, and justifying

Using inference and deduction skills

Solving problems

Making links between the clues

Making decisions

Speculating to form hypotheses

They should also be encouraged to use some of the following terms:

Inquire

Infer

Plan

Link or connect

Refine

Probable

Analyse

Hypothesise

Conclude

Data

Evidence

Possible

Sequence

Predict

Certain

1.9 USING THE PIT TOOLS

The learning activities in this book are designed to support you in your efforts to create rich, challenging learning opportunities at home. They are created in a way that allows for them to be equally as effective with one child and one adult or with multiple children and adults. They similarly work for a range of ages and can be done with a group of children of mixed age and ability.

You do not have to work through the activities in any particular order, nor do you need to use all of the pit tools within each theme. We have endeavoured to provide the broadest range of activities within each topic area, covering several subject areas, so that you can be selective in choosing which ones you feel would work best for your children. For example, if you have limited time on any evening, you could choose a short, practical activity to engage your children, whereas if you have a full day during school holidays, you may wish to focus on more lengthy and involved activities or those that require more setting up.

1.10 STAGE 4: CONSIDER

The final stage of a Learning Pit experience is for children to consider the learning journey they have been on and to look for ways to apply, adapt, and transfer their learning.

In his book *Unified Theories of Cognition*, Allen Newell (1991) points out that there are two layers of problem-solving: applying a strategy to the problem at hand and selecting and monitoring that strategy. Good problem-solving, Newell observes, often depends as much on the selection and monitoring of a strategy as it does on its execution. The term 'metacognition' (thinking about thinking) is commonly used to refer to selection and monitoring processes as well as to more general activities of reflecting on and directing one's own thinking. According to Newell, 'competent or successful learners can explain which strategies they used to solve a problem and why, whilst less competent students monitor their own thinking sporadically and ineffectively and offer incomplete explanations'(Newell, 1991, p. 312). The good news is that metacognitive strategies can be learned and continually developed. They are not something that children either have or don't have. They can be acquired in a methodical way to begin with and then be encouraged until eventually they become intellectual habits.

The following questions will help your children to develop their metacognitive habits. They are grouped according to the different stages of the Learning Pit. We are not advocating that you ask all of these! Instead, select two or three per section, and then vary the questions from session to session. We would also encourage you to share with your children why you are asking these questions and what you expect them to gain from the experience.

Stage 1: concept

1   Which concepts were most interesting?

2   What made these concepts better than others?

3   What was your first thought about these concepts?

4   How accurate did these early answers turn out to be?

5   How confident were you with your early answers?

6   How did your thinking affect the first steps on your learning journey?

Stage 2: conflict

1   Which two ideas formed the first cognitive conflict?

2   As you started to wobble, how did thàt make you feel?

3   Which two ideas conflicted the most and why?

4   Which ideas were dismissed easily and why?

5   Which skills of thinking did you use to analyse the conflict you felt in the pit?

6   Did you feel like giving up in the pit? If so, how did you resolve to keep going?

7   Do you feel as if you examined all the options when you were in the pit?

Stage 3: construct

1   When did you start to make sense of all the conflicting ideas you had in the pit?

2   Which was the most useful revelation you discovered?

3   Which thinking skills were most helpful in constructing your answer?

4   How sure can you be that you did not accept easy answers?

5   What misunderstandings, misconceptions, or assumptions did you uncover?

6   What did you do to check the accuracy of your answer?

7   If you had had time, what could you have done to improve your answer even further?

8   Do you feel satisfied with the learning journey you have been on?

Stage 4: consider

1   In what ways do you understand the concept better now?

2   What would you do differently next time?

3   Which strategies did you use this time that you could use in other contexts?

4   Is there a different sequence you could use next time to be more effective?

5   How could you adapt your new learning to another situation?

6   What analogy, metaphor, or example could you create to explain your new learning?

7   What advice would you give others about going through the Learning Pit?

8   What questions do you still have?

9   What is the next concept that you would like to explore?

1.11 FINAL POINTS ABOUT THE LEARNING PIT

1   Is the Learning Pit something to avoid?

Depends on the context, but ordinarily no – the Learning Pit is not something to be avoided. Of course, if you want a quick answer or resolution, then going into the Learning Pit is probably best avoided. But if you want your children to be more thoughtful about their answers, more aware of the possibilities and the problems, and more confident in the thoroughness of their understanding, then going into the Learning Pit is definitely worth the effort.

Furthermore, when you deliberately and strategically take children into the Learning Pit, they are likely to develop more resilience, gain greater self-efficacy, and build many of the strategies they will need for learning.

2   What age range does the Learning Pit work with?

If you think it appropriate to encourage a particular age group to step out of their comfort zone, then you could say that the Learning Pit is also relevant to them. The model has been used successfully with children between the ages of three and 19, as well as with adults. This book gives examples of using the Learning Pit across a wide age range, as does *The Learning Challenge* by James Nottingham (2017). *Challenging Early Learning* by Nottingham and Nottingham (2019) gives examples for three-to-seven-year-olds.

3   A Learning 'Pit' sounds negative; why can't it be a 'Mountain of Learning' instead?

James Nottingham chose a learning 'pit' because he wanted to be honest with his students: stepping out of your comfort zone makes you feel uncomfortable (there's a giveaway in the term!).

We understand why some people would prefer to use something like a 'mountain of learning', but our worry is that when someone reaches the top of a mountain, they have a sense of elation and accomplishment – which is certainly *not* what someone feels when faced with cognitive conflict. Learners tend to feel a sense of achievement at the *end* of the journey (when they've come out of the pit), not halfway through the journey (when they've reached the top of a mountain).

Thinking it through a little more, the learning journey we so often go on is one in which we move from (1) thinking we know what we're doing, to (2) realising we're not so sure because there's a lot of conflicting information to sift through, to (3) beginning to see some clarity as we sort and connect the new information, to (4) reflecting on what we've learned and how we've arrived at this point. If we were to use a 'mountain of learning' as our metaphor, then we'd complete all four stages of learning on the way up the mountain, begging the question 'what happens during the descent back down the mountain?'

Of course, it is not for us to say what metaphors people should use – that is entirely up to them and their children. On the other hand, we think it *is* okay for James Nottingham to say no, the Learning Pit (and all the ideas that go with it) should not be explained as a mountain of learning!

4   Should we help children climb out of the Learning Pit?

If the concept at the heart of the Learning Pit experience is one that you really need your children to know confidently, then yes – help them out of the pit. If, however, the concept is more obviously philosophical or open-ended and could help children to be more aware of context and caveats, then it is often better to give them the time and space to exit the pit in their own time.

For example, if the concept is a mathematical term such as 'fraction', 'number', 'ratio', or 'equal', then typically you would want to help children to climb out of the pit. That is not to say that the Learning Pit doesn't work in maths – in fact, it can work very well; nor is it to suggest by 'helping children out of the pit' that we mean you should do the work for them! You should still question, challenge, and engage children so that they have to work out how to get out of the pit themselves using the skills and strategies that they have developed.

On the other hand, if the concepts are more open-ended – for example, many of the concepts in literature, social interaction, history, geography, religion, and so on – then there are very often benefits to leaving children in the Learning Pit for days. Take, for example, bravery, freedom, justice, pace, pattern, shape, or growth – these concepts lend themselves to children thinking that on the one hand, the concept means X; at other times it means Y; and, with some exceptions or situations, it could mean Z. That is not to say we want children to be permanently confused, but it is to say there is a strength in being aware of the conditions and stipulations of each concept's application.

So, the quick answer is yes – help children climb out of the pit by guiding and encouraging them, and at other times, leave them in the Learning Pit so that they continue to wonder and investigate.

5   So, where do I start?

We recommend that you start with one or more of these options:

1.11.1 Talk through the purpose of the Learning Pit

- -

Share an image of the Learning Pit with your children (there are lots of options at www.ChallengingLearning.com/Learning-Pit), and tell them it shows what happens when learning something new. Use commentary along the lines of these statements:

> To begin with, you feel fairly confident that you know the answer or are able to perform the skill. However, once you start to investigate or try things further, you realise it's not as straightforward as you first thought. This means you are stepping out of your comfort zone, which in turn means you are learning. This is what we call going into the Learning Pit. It is when you have two or more ideas that you agree with, but which seem to be in conflict with each other. Don't worry, this 'conflict' is normal. In fact, if it *doesn't* happen, then you probably won't be able to make much progress.

> When you find yourself in the Learning Pit, look for connections, patterns or possibilities. This should help you begin to make more sense of the ideas or actions you are trying. Ask others for help. Offer advice to others. Work together to understand the problems and then find some solutions. As you build some clarity or confidence, this will take you out of the Learning Pit to a sense of eureka. When you achieve this eureka moment, you will know the effort has been worth it because you'll have a sense of achievement like no other.

> At the end of a Learning Pit journey, I will encourage you to think about what you've learned, which strategies you found most useful, and what you might do next time to make things even more successful for yourself and others.

1.11.2 Create a Learning Pit culture

- -

As you introduce the Learning Pit to children, remember to also bring the following attitudes with you:

- I am interested in and respect your ideas.

- I will show interest by listening to you, questioning you, and encouraging you to elaborate.

- I am confident you are capable of coming up with relevant questions, opinions, reasons, examples, and comparisons.

- I will base our dialogue as much as I can on your questions, understanding, interests, and values.

- We are thinkers who can tackle questions together and work towards the best answers and understanding.
- You should feel secure enough to take intellectual risks.
- Going through the Learning Pit leads to deeper and more enduring understanding.

REFERENCES

Bjork, E. L., & Bjork, R. A. (2011). Making things hard on yourself, but in a good way: Creating desirable difficulties to enhance learning. *Psychology and the Real World: Essays Illustrating Fundamental Contributions to Society*, 2, 59–68.

Moser, J. S., Schroder, H. S., Heeter, C., Moran, T. P., & Lee, Y.-H. (2011). Mind your errors: Evidence for a neural mechanism linking growth mindset to adaptive post-error adjustments. *Psychological Science*, 22, 1484–1489.

Newell, A. (1991). *Unified theories of cognition*. Cambridge, MA: Harvard University Press.

Nottingham, J. A. (2017). *The learning challenge: How to guide your students through the learning pit*. Thousand Oaks, CA: Corwin.

Nottingham, J. A., & Nottingham, J. (2019). *Challenging early learning: Helping young children learn how to learn*. London and New York: Routledge.

Rowe, M. B. (1986). Wait time: Slowing down may be a way of speeding up! *Journal of Teacher Education*, 37(1), 43–50.

Vygotsky, L. (1978). *Mind and society*. Cambridge, MA: Harvard University Press.

Wiliam, D. (2016, April 28). Learning styles: What does the research say? [Blog post]. Retrieved from http://deansforimpact.org/post_Learning_styles_what_does_the_ research_say.html

Yair, G. (2000). Reforming motivation: How the structure of instruction affects students' learning experiences. *British Educational Research Journal*, 26, 191–210.

PART 2. LESSONS TO SUPPORT LEARNING THROUGH THE PIT

2. LESSONS ABOUT OURSELVES

LESSON 1 BIG QUESTION – WHAT IS CHOICE?

Dinner table conversations

Concept: Choice

Main question: What does it mean to choose?

Follow-up questions:

- Is it good to have choices?
- How do you know what to choose and what not to choose?
- Do we all have the same choices?
- How do you know if you have a choice to make?
- How does it feel when you make a choice?
- What makes some choices easy and some difficult?
- Does making choices get easier as you get older?
- How old do you need to be before you can make a choice?

Concept: Choice

Main question: Can we have too many choices?

Follow-up questions:

- How much choice is enough?
- What does it mean to have free choice?
- Do we always want more choices than we have?
- Will more choice improve the quality of the decision we make?
- When does choice become stressful?
- When does choice give us freedom?
- Can we share our choices with others?
- Should we always make our own choices?
- When should we allow other people to choose for us?
- Is it ever possible to have no choice at all?
- How would you feel if only people with brown eyes had the right to choose?

Concept: Choice

Main question: Do all choices have consequences?

Follow-up questions:

- Do better choices always lead to better outcomes?
- What is the difference between choices and consequences?
- How do the choices we make change us?
- Who decides if the consequences of our choices are positive or negative?
- If you are free to choose, are you also free of the consequences of that choice?
- Does having choice always mean also having responsibility?
- What influences the choices we make?

Concept: Choice

Main question: Is there such a thing as the 'right' choice?

Follow-up questions:

- What makes something the right choice?
- What is the difference between a choice and a right choice?
- How do we know what the right choice is?
- How should you feel when making the right choice?
- Should we always make the right choice?
- Is there always just one right choice?
- What if there was no such thing as the right choice?
- Is it possible to always make the right choice?
- Is it possible to always know what the right choice is?
- Who decides what is the right choice or not?

Picture book activity

You Choose by Nick Sharratt and Pippa Goodhart is a good book to discuss the concept of choice.

You can access a YouTube version of the book. Pause it on each page and discuss the question posed.

www.youtube.com/watch?v=4x9B0uMeyQM

Tic-tac-toe / Noughts and crosses

Play tic-tac-toe / noughts and crosses on paper, a dry erase board, or using chalk outside. Ask your children why they make the choice about where to place an X or O. Share your thinking about your choices as well.

This variation was shared by Marilyn Burns in her blog: www.marilynburnsmathblog.com/five-twists-on-tic-tac-toe/.

What's the *same* as playing the regular game is that you take turns as you usually do. What's *different* is that you don't start by deciding who is X and who is O. Instead, on your turn, you may write either an X or an O in any empty square, and you can change your mind from turn to turn. So can your opponent. The winner is the same as in the regular game – whoever completes a row with three Xs or three Os wins – whether or not that player actually wrote them all.

Group game – number roulette

Outside, use chalk to make a 3 x 4 grid and write the numbers 2–12 in 11 of the squares and the word 'DOUBLE' in the 12th square.

- For each turn, each person selects a square to stand in.
- One person rolls two dice.
- If anyone is standing in the square that is the sum of the two numbers, they get one point.
- If a double is rolled and someone is standing on 'double', they get two points.
- Repeat until someone scores ten points.

Group game – place value choice

Use index cards or pieces of paper to create ten cards and write the numbers 0–9 (one number per card) on them. The object of the game is to make the highest three-digit number possible.

- Each person in the family has their own sheet of paper or white board and draws three lines like this: ___ ___ ___.
- Draw one card – everyone must decide whether they want that number in the 1s place, the 10s place, or the 100s place.
- Repeat two more times, then compare numbers.
- You can increase the difficulty by trying four-digit numbers.

Talk about

- how you decided where to put each number;
- what made the decision more or less difficult;
- whether it would be more or less difficult if you return the cards to the pile each time;
- whether or not it is a choice to put the 0 in the 100s spot and what that means.

Fairy tale choices – 'The Three Little Pigs'

Share the story 'The Three Little Pigs' with your children. There are many versions out there aimed at all age ranges as well as animations and dramatisations of the story, and any will work. The following are two YouTube versions that you may use:

Animated: www.youtube.com/watch?v=-gdcgnSrUvU&t=226s

Traditional book-based: www.youtube.com/watch?v=1WjHqT8dgeQ

Alternative versions to explore are

The True Story of the Three Little Pigs (Scieska 1989) and

The Three Little Wolves and the Big Bad Pig (Trivias 1993).

After sharing the story, work with your child/ren to identify all the choices within the story.

Examples may include the following:

- *The little pigs choose to leave their mother's home to make their own way in the world.*
- *They choose to live separately from each other.*
- *One little pig chooses straw to build his house.*
- *One little pig chooses sticks to build his house.*
- *One little pig chooses bricks to build his house.*
- *The pigs choose not to work together or share ideas.*
- *Each pig chooses to be different from the others.*
- *All the pigs choose to see the wolf as dangerous and their enemy.*
- *All pigs choose not to ask the wolf what he might want.*
- *The first pig chooses not to let the wolf into his house.*
- *The first pig chooses to run to the second pig's house because it is closest.*
- *Pig #2 chooses not to let the wolf into his house.*
- *Pigs #1 and #2 choose to run to Pig #3's house together.*
- *Pig #3 chooses not to let the wolf into his house.*
- *Pig #3 chooses to trick the wolf.*
- *The Three Little Pigs choose violence and revenge as a way of dealing with the wolf.*

Questions to explore the theme of choice in the story:

- *Why do you think the Three Little Pigs chose the building materials they did?*
- *Who do you think made the best choices in the story? Why?*
- *What makes some choices better than others?*
- *What other choices of building materials could the pigs make?*
- *What choices did the wolf make?*
- *What do you think are the most important things the pigs should think about when choosing their building materials?*
- *How do we know if a choice is a safe one or not?*

- *What might be the impact of not thinking carefully about the choices we make?*
- *What can we learn from this story about making choices?*
- *What choices do you have to make each day?*

Concept target

Together with your child/ren, create a list of vocabulary related to the concept of choice.

Here is a list of related vocabulary to start you off using the concept target. It would be great if you and your child could add to this list or make your own list. Remember to draw on your discussions from some of the other activities to help to evaluate each word or term.

- Choice
- Decision
- Impact
- Influence
- Control
- Consequence
- Outcome
- Responsibility

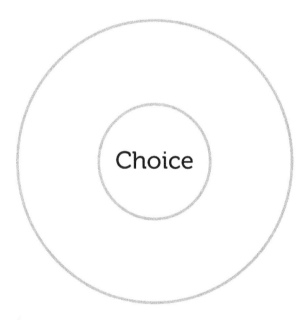

Growth mindset goal spinner

Make a wheel of fortune like the following example. You can use a paper plate: fold it in half and then into thirds, and cut each rounded edge off between the folds to make a hexagon. Have your children choose six goals that they have over the few months and write them in each section. Make sure the goals they write are achievable and their progress towards them is measurable. For example:

Goal: To be able to draw better animals

Action: Watch a weekly online tutorial and practice. Keep drawings as you go along to show improvement.

Poke a hole in the centre of the hexagon and push a pencil, tip first through the hole to make a spinner. Each day, spin and see where it lands in order to help you choose which goal to focus on when.

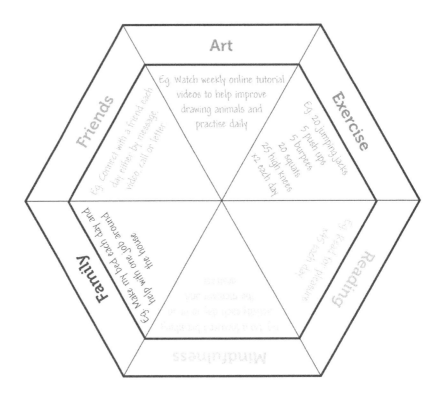

Would you rather?

Use the following cards to challenge everyone in your family to make difficult choices. Cut the cards up and choose them randomly or just read them off of the sheet. Ask each other questions like the following:

- Why did you choose that?
- Would you always choose that one? What might change your mind?
- What are the advantages of each? What are the disadvantages of each?
- Can you think of someone who would choose differently than you? Why?

Would you rather...	Would you rather...	Would you rather...
Live in the city or the countryside?	Be an inventor or an explorer?	Go to school 5 days for 6 hours per day or go to school 3 days for 10 hour per day?
©2020 www.challenginglearning.com	©2020 www.challenginglearning.com	©2020 www.challenginglearning.com

Would you rather...	Would you rather...	Would you rather...
Visit the past or the future?	Be a wild animal or a family pet?	Have lots of casual friends or one really good best friend?
©2020 www.challenginglearning.com	©2020 www.challenginglearning.com	©2020 www.challenginglearning.com
Would you rather...	Would you rather...	Would you rather...
Be an adult or a child?	Make all of your own choices or have others choose for you?	Be in love and have your heart broken or never be in love at all?
©2020 www.challenginglearning.com	©2020 www.challenginglearning.com	©2020 www.challenginglearning.com
Would you rather...	Would you rather...	Would you rather...
Discover something new in space or something new on Earth?	Be an expert on human behaviour or an expert on animal behavior?	Climb a mountain or dive to the bottom of the ocean?
©2020 www.challenginglearning.com	©2020 www.challenginglearning.com	©2020 www.challenginglearning.com

Would you rather...	Would you rather...	Would you rather...
Plant a tree or read a book?	Be a part of a team or work on your own?	Be the best player on a team that always loses or the best player on a team that always wins?
©2020 www.challenginglearning.com	©2020 www.challenginglearning.com	©2020 www.challenginglearning.com
Would you rather...	Would you rather...	Would you rather...
Always get really easy schoolwork or get schoolwork that challenges you to think?	Be a follower or a leader?	Have 4 brothers or 4 sisters?
©2020 www.challenginglearning.com	©2020 www.challenginglearning.com	©2020 www.challenginglearning.com
Would you rather...	Would you rather...	
Travel around the world or stay in the comfort of your home?	Be famous for doing something bad or have nobody know who you are?	
©2020 www.challenginglearning.com	©2020 www.challenginglearning.com	

 Lessons to support learning

Folklore – choices

Read *Mufaro's Beautiful Daughters* by John Steptoe. It can be found in a library, a bookstore, or online. Then use the questions following the story to discuss the choices in this story.

- When do you think the king decided that Nyasha was his choice to be his queen?

- Why was it the king's choice as to who would be queen?

- How much choice do you think Nyasha had about becoming queen?

- Who had the most choice in this story, the men or the women? Why?

- Does the ability to choose always come with having power?

- Was the king right to choose to trick Mufaro's daughters?

- Has Manyara's right to choose been taken away from her by making her the queen's servant?

- What are the key differences in they way that Mufaro and Nyasha chose to live their lives?

- What motivated Mufaro to make the choices she made?

- What motivated Nyasha to make the choices she made?

- Does making good choices always lead to good outcomes?

- How would the story change if Nyasha did not choose to feed the hungry boy or thank the old woman?

- How much were all the characters aware of the choices they were making?

- If you are not consciously aware of making a choice, is it no longer a choice?

Venn diagram with *Mufaro's Beautiful Daughters* and 'Cinderella'

Review the fairy tale 'Cinderella' and compare and contrast the two stories. Think about what happened in each story and try to find the ways that they are similar and different. Draw two circles on a piece of paper like the ones that follow to categorise your ideas.

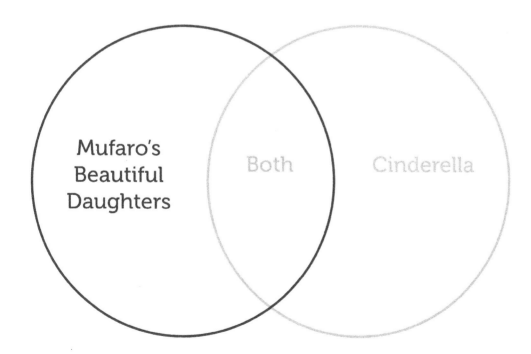

Choose your own adventure

Family style

As a family, create a story with input from everyone in the family.

- Sit in a circle.
- Start with one person who provides the first word or the first sentence for a story.
- Move to the next person and have them add on. Encourage fun and silliness, but try to make sense.
- Keep going until you feel like your story has come to end, or you can set a certain number of times to go around the circle.
- Be sure to have someone recording the story or taking notes.
- Write or type the story and then on another day you can illustrate it.

Kitchen style

Let your child choose three to four ingredients that you already have in the house. Then work together to create a meal using all of the ingredients (plus more if needed).

Talk about why your children chose the ingredients they did, whether they would think about different ingredients the next time, and what they found to be the most challenging about the ingredients they chose.

STEM activity: egg drop design

Collect items like cotton balls, Ziploc bags, paper towels, Styrofoam, plastic, pipe cleaners, yarn cardboard, etc. for your child to use to create a container that will protect an egg when dropped.

- Tell your child/ren that they may choose three items to use to create a container that will protect an egg from a six-foot / two-metre drop.
- Encourage them to think about and draw their design before choosing their items.
- Once they choose their items, have them make their container using just those items (you can decide if they automatically receive tape or glue).
- When they are done, test them out by standing on a chair and measuring 6 feet from the floor to the drop point.

Talk about what happened and ask questions like these:

- Would you choose different items if you tried again? Why or why not?
- What do you think worked well? What could you have done better?
- What might you change about your design if you tried it again?

Fortune teller story

Use the following directions to create and label your story fortune teller. Once you have created your fortune teller and have determined a setting, main character, and plot, write your own story. Try to include difficult choices that your character(s) have to make.

Making your story fortune teller . . .

1. Get a piece of A4 paper

2. Fold bottom right corner over the left hand side of the paper to make an equilateral triangle

3. Cut off the excess paper of the top of the triangle

4. Unfold the triangle so that you are left with a square

5. Take the bottom corner and fold it up to the top corner to create another triangle

6. Unfold so you are left with quarter folds in the paper square

7. Take each corner and fold into the centre point

8. Continue this until all corners are folded into the centre

9. Turn paper over to show a square

10. Fold each corner into the centre point again

11. Continue this until all corners are folded into the centre

12. Fold the square as you see it in half

Instructions for adding story settings and using the story fortune teller

Open up your story fortune teller and add the details in the following picture (then later, make up your own details to create a NEW story fortune teller).

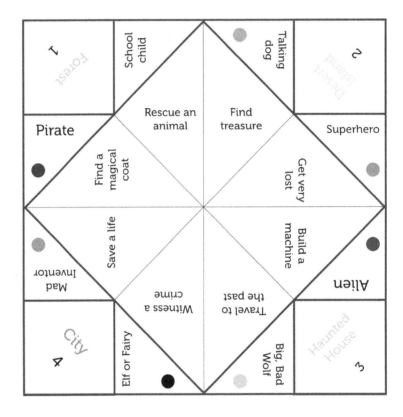

Then . . .

1 Choose your story setting. Write it down.

2 Move the fortune teller how many times the number next to the setting you chose says.

3 Now choose your main character. Write this down.

4 Move the fortune teller according to how many letters there are in the colour of the dot next to the character you chose, for example, red dot = three moves.

5 Now choose your plot by choosing a colour and opening that flap. Write this down.

6 Now you have a setting, a character, and a plot, and you are ready to get creative and start writing your story. Have fun!

Guess my number

Write a number on a piece of paper and fold it in half.

- Encourage your child/ren to work out what the number is by asking questions using mathematical vocab.
- You can only answer yes or no.
- You can set it up like hangman where they only have so many chances before the game is over.

Assist your child/ren with using the following terms/phrases:

Bigger than, smaller than, greater than, less than, multiple of, divisible by, square number, cube number, prime number, odd, even, whole number, fraction, decimal, negative number, in the x times table, has x number of digits, within the range of x and y, etc.

Rock painting maths

Add some fun activity to mental maths by painting some rocks in bright colours and numbering them 0–10. You can also paint rocks to represent the four number operations, addition, subtraction, multiplication, and division. Using plastic hoops or hoops made from knotted pieces of string, throw them over the rocks to see what number combinations and calculations you come up with. To mix it up, throw a die first to determine how many hoop throws you get each round. For example:

Die shows four hoop throws

Two hoops around 10 = 20

One hoop around x (multiplication)

One hoop around 2

So 20 x 2 = 40

Lessons to support learning

LESSON 2 BIG QUESTION – WHAT IS HAPPINESS?

Idea One:
You can tell when
someone is happy

Idea Two:
People often pretend
to be happy when
they are not

Dinner table conversations

Concept: Happiness

Main question: What is happiness?

Follow-up questions:

- How do you know if you are happy?
- How do you know if others are happy?
- Can you always tell if someone is happy?
- Do we all experience happiness in the same way?
- Is happiness a personal experience?
- Can happiness be shared with others?
- Who decides what happiness is?
- Do happy people have more friends, or does having more friends make you happier?

Concept: Happiness

Main question: Can you measure happiness?

Follow-up questions:

- Is happiness always a positive emotion?
- Can happiness ever be negative?

- What is the cost of happiness?

- How much happiness is enough?

- What amount of happiness would be too little?

- How long does happiness last?

- Is happiness always temporary?

- Do you need to have experienced sadness in order to know happiness?

- How much sadness do you need to have experienced in order to appreciate happiness?

Concept: Happiness

Main question: Should we all aim for happiness?

Follow-up questions:

- Does everyone want to be happy?

- Is it ever pointless to try and be happy?

- Would it be wrong to be happy all of the time?

- What if our happiness makes someone else sad?

- What is the difference between pleasure and happiness?

- When might the desire to be happy become a stress that makes us sad?

- How important is happiness?

- How important is sadness compared to happiness?

- Should the pursuit of happiness be a life-long challenge?

Concept: Happiness

Main question: How much are we in control of our own happiness?

Follow-up questions:

- Can you choose to make yourself happy?

- Can you choose to make other people happy?

- How much do other people and things around you influence your happiness?

- Is happiness contagious?

- Do you think we are born happy or that happiness is something we have to learn?

- What is the difference between being happy with yourself and being happy with life?

- Is there a secret to finding happiness?

- Is total happiness even achievable?

Picture book activity

- -

The Red Tree by Shaun Tan is a good book to discuss the concept of happiness being worth the wait.

You can access a plan that includes a link to a YouTube version here: www.challenginglearning. com/wp-content/uploads/2020/03/9-14_The-Red-Tree.pdf.

Pay it forward – make others happy

- -

Think of ways that you could make other people happy. Send a card, drop off flowers, send a picture, etc. Do some of these things and ask people to keep it going by doing something for someone else to make them happy.

Put messages in your window or write them with sidewalk chalk to make people happy when they pass your house.

Happy favourites

Talk about your favourite numbers, shapes, and colours, and think about whether they make you happy.

What is your favourite number?

What makes it your favourite?

Does it make you happy? Why?

Are some numbers happier numbers than others?

Do positive numbers make us feel happier than negative numbers?

What about square numbers or prime numbers?

What about shapes and colours?

What shapes do you identify as happy shapes?

Do some colours make you more happy than others? Why?

Happy numbers

In mathematics, there is a theory that there are happy numbers and unhappy numbers.

To find out if a number is happy you have to square each digit, add the answers together, and repeat until the number equals 1 (happy number) or loops endlessly producing numbers that do not equal 1 (unhappy numbers). For example, take the number 23:

$$23$$
$$2^2 = 4$$
$$3^2 = 9$$
$$4 + 9 = 13$$
$$1^2 = 1$$
$$3^2 = 9$$
$$1 + 9 = 10$$
$$1^2 = 1$$
$$0^2 = 0$$
$$1 + 0 = 1$$

So, 23, 13, and 10 are happy numbers!

There are 20 happy numbers between 1 and 100. We have listed three of them; how many more can you find?

The Pig of Happiness

Share *The Pig of Happiness* by Edward Monkton with your child. It can be found in a bookstore, a library, or online. Here is a link to a YouTube version: www.youtube.com/watch?v=uoilYlww8M4.

The Pig of Happiness uses a literary device called an 'allegory' – a story or picture with a hidden, deeper meaning, delivering a message about real-world issues.

Here are some of the real-world issues included in the story *The Pig of Happiness*. Discuss and explore these with your child/ren to understand the idea or principle better. Together, can you identify any other issues in the story?

Idea 1 – We can be happy ALL of the time.
- Is it healthy to be happy all of the time?
- If we never feel sadness, how do we know if we are happy or not?
- Have you ever been happy all of the time?
- How did you know you were happy?

Idea 2 – Complaining and grumbling is wrong.
- If you are unhappy about something, should you keep it to yourself?
- Would keeping your complaints to yourself make you happy?
- Can you complain and be happy at the same time?
- How could complaining have a positive outcome?
- When was the last time you complained? How did you feel?

Idea 3 – Having a happy state of mind most of the time isn't ordinary or normal (it's extraordinary).
- What is a normal balance of emotions?

- Is it good for our health to have both positive and negative feelings?
- How could trying to be extraordinary in this way be dangerous?

Idea 4 – You can have too much happiness.
- Can too much happiness make you unhappy?
- How could being too happy stop us from taking risks or going on adventures or looking for other possibilities to make the world a better place?
- How could being too happy leave us vulnerable to danger?
- How much happiness is too much?

Idea 5 – Our happiness is dependent upon our view of things.
- If we decide to be a 'happy person', does that make us a happy person?
- Can every experience be turned into a happy one?
- Do we need to know what happiness looks like in order to be happy?
- How much do the things we have and the objects around us make us happy?
- What makes you happiest?

Idea 6 – In the end everyone should be happy (even chickens).
- What would the world be like if everyone was happy all the time?
- Would this 'happiness' be real?
- Does everyone have the potential to be happy?

Idea 7 – We have to change ourselves first before we can influence others.
- How important is it that we model the behaviour ourselves that we expect from others?
- What are the positives and negatives of comparing yourself to others?
- What makes someone a good leader or influencer of others?
- Can anyone be influenced by an effective leader?

Idea 8 – We can change other people's thinking and behaviour by how we behave ourselves.
- Is it really possible to spread happiness?
- Is it good to change other people's thoughts and behaviour?
- What was the last thing you did to cheer someone up?
- How could we control whether this change was positive or negative?

Happiness jar

Create a happiness jar to store some of your happy thoughts.

- Each day put in one thing that made you feel happy during the day.
- Put a date on each slip so that when you read back you can remember the occasion.
- Decorate the jar and hang on to it for the next year.

After a year, plan to look through the slips and think about the following:

- Do you think you will remember those things happening? Which ones do you think you will remember the most? Why?
- How might your idea of what makes you happy be different in a year when you read them?

Happiness poetry

Write a poem about happiness. It could be an acrostic poem using the letters H-A-P-P-I-N-E-S-S. For example:

Happiness is . . .

Having fun with my friends

Amazing adventures

Playing on my bike

Painting colourful pictures

Ice cream and chocolate

Nice sunny days

Enjoying cuddles

Swimming on holidays

Sledging in the snow

Lessons to support learning

OR

It could be a haiku (a short Japanese poem consisting of three short lines that do not rhyme: The first line is five syllables. The second line is seven syllables. The third line is five syllables like the first. Punctuation and capitalisation are up to the poet and need not follow the rigid rules used in structuring sentences). For example:

Happiness is real

Makes you feel warm and fuzzy

Embrace it and smile.

Concept target

Together with your child/ren, create a list of vocabulary related to the concept of happiness.

Here is a list of related vocabulary to start you off using the concept target. It would be great if you and your child could add to this list or make your own list. Remember to draw on your discussions from some of the other activities to help to evaluate each word or term.

- Joy
- Emotion
- Experience
- Positivity
- Contentment
- Pleasure
- Cheerfulness
- Mindfulness

Happy art

Artists choose their colours very carefully to reflect the mood of their paintings and the characters within them. Between 1901 and 1904 Picasso famously went through his 'blue' period where he painted only in shades of blue and blue-green to reflect the sadness and despair he felt in his personal life.

If you were wanting to reflect happiness in your paintings and had to choose one colour that you felt summed up happiness, what would it be? Why does that colour represent happiness for you? Try producing some pieces of art work that only use shades of your 'happy colour'. You could use paint, pencils, or chalk or create a collage using pieces of paper all in the one colour. Display them somewhere special to make you feel happy.

Would you be happiest?

Use the following cards to challenge everyone in your family to make difficult choices. Cut the cards up and choose them randomly or just read them off of the sheet. Ask each other questions like these:

- Why did you choose that?
- Would you always choose that one? What might change your mind?
- What are the advantages of each? What are the disadvantages of each?
- Can you think of someone who would choose differently than you? Why?

Would you be happiest...	Would you be happiest...	Would you be happiest...
Dancing or singing?	Being 5 years older or 2 years younger?	Being a famous artist or a famous writer?
©2020 www.challenginglearning.com	©2020 www.challenginglearning.com	©2020 www.challenginglearning.com

Would you be happiest...

Would you be happiest...

Would you be happiest...

Working by yourself or working as part of a team?

Living in the middle of a forest or living by the seaside?

Being rich but unknown or famous but poor?

Would you be happiest...

Would you be happiest...

Would you be happiest...

Having lots of siblings or being an only child?

Eating an apple or an orange?

Playing outdoors or indoors?

Would you be happiest...

Would you be happiest...

Would you be happiest...

Owning a dog or a cat?

Riding a bike or riding a horse?

Having no homework or no tests?

Would you be happiest...

Would you be happiest...

Would you be happiest...

Eating an endless supply of chocolate or an endless supply of ice-cream?

Moving to your dream house or going on your dream holiday?

Travelling by car or travelling by plane?

Would you be happiest...   Would you be happiest...   Would you be happiest...

Roller skating or water   Having a cosy evening   Reading the book or
skiing?   in your house or a fun   watching the film of
                                  night out in town?   the book?

©2020 www.challenginglearning.com ©2020 www.challenginglearning.com ©2020 www.challenginglearning.com

Would you be happiest...   Would you be happiest...

Giving someone a   Having 5 of your
present they have   favourite things to
always wanted or   share with someone
receiving a present you   else or having only
have always wanted?   2 of your favourite
                                  things but having them
                                  to yourself?

©2020 www.challenginglearning.com ©2020 www.challenginglearning.com

Why does symmetry make us feel happy?

Most objects in the real world are symmetrical, especially in nature. The petals on a flower, a butterfly's wings, a starfish, snowflakes, spiders' webs, a hexagonal honeycomb – these are just some of the many examples of symmetry in the natural world. We as human beings and our animal friends are, on the surface also examples of symmetry.

Why do we get a sense of pleasure from looking at things that are symmetrical? Why do we like to watch synchronised swimmers or water swirling down a plug hole?

Symmetry is a form of mathematics that is a type of secret language or code that helps to keep the natural world in balance and harmony and gives us a sense of organisation and order. Humans and animals are naturally attracted to symmetry. For example, the bumble bee has very poor eyesight but can recognise symmetrical shapes, and because flowers are symmetrical, the bee can find them and carry out its important role in pollination. Similarly, a peacock fans his tail feathers to attract a mate and creates a wonderful display of vibrant symmetry. Symmetry has become a hugely important feature in art, architecture, and music because of how it gives us pleasure and makes us feel happy.

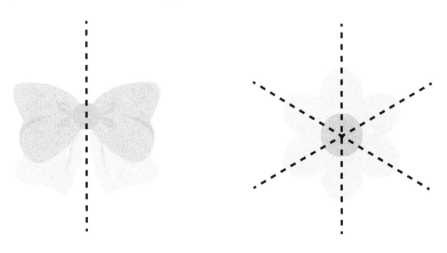

Symmetry scavenger hunt

Go on a 'symmetry scavenger hunt' and record all the different examples of symmetry around you, both in natural and in man-made form. You could also look through books for examples.

Examples would include the following:

- A ladybird's wings
- Insects
- Fruit cut down the centre (e.g., strawberries, oranges, apples)
- Leaf shapes and patterns
- Flower petals
- Pair of scissors
- A spider's web
- Windows
- Our skeleton
- Faces
- A balance weighing scale
- A peacock's open tail feathers

More symmetry

- Which letters of the alphabet have at least one line of symmetry? Which ones have more than one line of symmetry? Does it matter how you write them?
- Which numbers have at least one line of symmetry? Does it matter how you write them?
- Create your own symmetry: Fold a piece of paper in half, then, using the folded line as your line of symmetry, see how many symmetrical patterns/pictures you can make. Use a mirror to check your accuracy.
- Use sidewalk chalk to draw symmetrical shapes for others to enjoy.

Graphing happiness

Have your child/ren make a list of five to ten things that make them happy. Then, for each item, have them rank their level of happiness from 1 to 10, with 1 being 'not happy / no feeling' and 10 being 'extreme happiness', for each of the following:

- how they felt while waiting for it to happen/arrive
- how they felt while it was happening / once it arrived
- how they felt the day after it happened/arrived
- how they felt the week after it happened/arrived

For example, if what makes them happy is going to the park, then they might have high numbers for the first two but low numbers for the last two, but if what makes them happy is receiving a gift, they might have all high numbers.

Use the graph that follows to graph each of the happiness moments, each in a different colour. Then discuss, using questions like these:

- What do you notice? What do you think that means?
- Are the lines that don't drop at the end things that make you happier?
- What is the difference between the lines that drop down at the end and the ones that do not?
- What are some other examples of things that make you happy that would look like [pick a line] this one?

Happiness Graph

Choose a different colour pen/marker/pencil for each of the things that make you happy. Start with one of the them and mark with a dot your level of happiness for each time period, then connect the dots. Move to the next colour and keep going until you have graphed all of the things that make you happy.

Level of Happiness	While waiting for it to happen/arrive	While it is happening/Once it has arrived	The day after it happens/arrives	A week after it happens/arrives
10				
9				
8				
7				
6				
5				
4				
3				
2				
1				

Venn diagram with happiness

Have everyone in the family brainstorm some of the things that make them happy. Share them and create a Venn diagram comparing and contrasting the things that make adults happy with the things that make children happy.

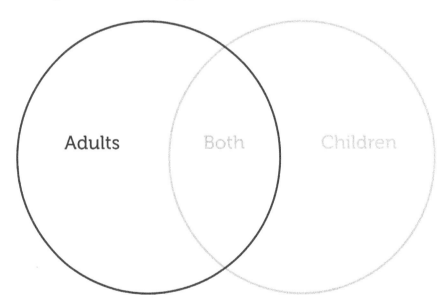

Mindfulness

Mindfulness involves being present in the moment without judgement or distractions. It is a time to be aware of thoughts and feelings and accept them in a calm way. It helps to build and maintain happiness because it can help to reduce stress and anxiety. Try some of these activities to help your child practice mindfulness.

Three deep breaths

Use this script to guide your child to take three deep breaths:

Find a comfortable seat.

I invite you to close your eyes. You can also take a soft gaze at the floor, if that feels better.

Put your spine in a line. Place one hand over your heart. Put the other hand over top.

Take a deep breath in. Open your mouth and let it go. Breath in, fill up your whole belly. Sigh it out. One more breath in, the biggest breath of the day. Breath out, release.

Talk with your children about how the three breaths make them feel:

- Do you feel different after you take three deep breaths?

- When might it be a good idea for you to stop and take the time to take three deep breaths?

The Sound of Silence

YouTube version: www.youtube.com/watch?v=h3h7TRtoR4Q

This book by Katrina Goldsaito encourages children to stop and think about all of the sounds that they hear and introduces the idea of *ma* or 'the sound of silence'. Read this book or watch it on YouTube and then take time to listen.

- Find a comfortable spot.

- Turn off televisions, radios, phones, or anything else that may add extra sounds.

- Set a timer for five minutes and then spend that time just listening with eyes closed.

After five minutes, talk about what you heard or didn't hear:

- What sounds did you hear? How did they make you feel?

- Were there moments where you 'heard' silence?

- Which sounds do you not normally hear?

Two-word check-in

Try this in the morning or just before you do an activity together to focus your child on their emotions and provide them with a time of reflection.

- Say a word and tell your child to give you the first two words that come to mind. It is helpful if the word you choose is somehow related to your current situation. For example, if you are about to take a walk, use the word 'walk', or if you are going to read a book, use 'story' or 'reading'.

- Do not question them, reflect them, or evaluate them, just accept them and move on to another word.

Mindful activities

Choose activities throughout the day that allow for mindfulness:

- Colouring

- Playing

- Singing and dancing

- Origami

- Yoga poses described as animals

- Sleeping lions game – children lie on the floor as still and quiet as possible, like a lion napping

Other activities

Word scavenger hunt

Go on a word scavenger hunt with your child. Identify a certain sound, like 'oo' in 'b<u>oo</u>k' and 'h<u>oo</u>k', or 'tch' like in 'wa<u>tch</u>' and 'pa<u>tch</u>'.

- Set goals, like finding at least ten words, and see if you can reach or even beat your goal.

- Race each other through the house or go outside and see who can find five words first.

- Challenge your child to go on the scavenger hunt on their own and draw and label pictures of what they find (while you relax for a moment ☺).

- Find ten objects that have the same sound and see if your child can figure out the sound just by looking at the objects.

Measurement fun

Create measuring tapes using your own units of measure (hand, foot, finger) on a long strip of paper or paper that is taped together. Have multiple people in the family create their own measuring tape.

Now measure items around the house or outside using your measuring tape, and record your measurements. Find something to measure that is longer than your measuring tape and have your child figure out what to do.

Discuss the following:

Does it matter that our measurements do not come out the same? Why or why not?

Why are they different?

Why do you think we use standard measurements (like metres, feet, centimetres, inches)?

LESSON 3 BIG QUESTION – WHAT IS A DREAM?

Idea One:
Dreaming is something I do when I'm asleep

Idea Two:
I often dream when I'm awake about things I'd like to do

Dreams

STRONGER LEARNING for **STRONGER LIVES**

Dinner table conversations

Concept: Dreams

Main question: What is a dream?

Follow-up questions:

- Is there a difference between a dream and a nightmare?
- Are daydreams still dreams?
- Do you need to be asleep to dream?
- Do you know when you are dreaming?
- How can you be sure that you have stopped dreaming?
- What is the difference between dreamtime and awake time?
- Do dreams repeat themselves?
- Do animals dream?
- Can you control your dreams?
- How do your day-to-day experiences affect your dreams?
- At what age do we start dreaming?
- Are we able to dream even before we are born?

Concept: Dreams

Main question: Why do we dream?

Follow-up questions:

- Are dreams meaningless?
- What is the connection between our dreams and our emotions?
- How do you feel if you wake up remembering a good dream?
- How do you feel if you wake up from a nightmare?
- Can our dreams help us to deal with our reality?
- Do only people with very active imaginations dream?
- Do you have more interesting dreams if you have a creative imagination?
- Do we only daydream if we are bored?
- Do some people have more dreams than others?
- Do we dream differently across the world?
- Do dreams improve our memories?

Concept: Dreams

Main question: Is it good to dream?

Follow-up questions:

- Is dreaming good for our health?
- Are we responsible for our dreams?
- Can our dreams inspire us to achieve great things?
- Could our dreams influence our lives in a negative way?
- If dreaming allows us to escape reality, is that a good or a bad thing?
- How much do you think our dreams reflect our real thoughts and desires?
- Does doing something bad in your dreams mean you are a bad person in reality?
- What do our dreams tell us about our character?

Concept: Dreams

Main question: Can we learn from our dreams?

Follow-up questions:

- If you practice a new skill in your dream, could it help you improve that skill in reality?
- Could your dreams reveal answers to you that you have been struggling to find?
- Can our dreams help us to predict the future?
- How much do our dreams reveal our true thoughts and feelings to us?
- Can dreams ever really come true?
- Is it possible to teach yourself things in your dreams?
- How might dreams help us to organise and make sense of all the things on our mind?
- How powerful are your dreams in influencing your awake thoughts and actions?
- If you could learn anything through a dream, what would it be and why?

Dreams – fact or myth

Many people have studied dreams in order to understand why we have them, how they are developed, and how they affect us. Over the years, there have been many statements about dreams that have been shared yet have been shown to be false. Talk with your child about the difference between a fact and a myth:

Fact = a thing that is known or proven to be true

Myth = a false belief or idea

The following cards have some interesting statements about dreams. Can you sort the facts from the myths? The answers are also listed so that you can check your thinking. How many of the 21 do you think you will get right?

Everybody dreams.	Most of our dreams are forgotten.	Males and females dream differently.
Animals don't dream.	Blind people can only dream in sounds.	Everyone's dreams are completely different.
If you snore more, then you dream more.	Dreams can predict future health problems.	People who stay up late at night have more nightmares.
All dreams are in colour.	Dreams are mainly positive emotional experiences.	You can't control your dreams.
It is dangerous if your muscles relax too much while you are dreaming.	Six years of your lifetime is spent dreaming.	Scientists are clear about the role of dreams.
We mainly dream in pictures.	Most dreams are totally random.	Dreaming shuts our brains down.
We can only see faces we already know when we dream.	Dreams help us solve puzzles.	Less sleep means more intense dreams.

Questions to consider:

- How did you decide which statement was a fact and which one was a myth?
- Were some statements more obvious facts/myths than others?
- Could you make a decision about every statement or did you have an 'unsure' pile?
- Which statements surprised you? Why?
- What have you discovered while doing this activity that you didn't know before?

Dreams – fact or myth – answers

Everybody dreams. **(fact)**

Adults and babies alike dream for around two hours every night. Each dream usually lasts for between five and 20 minutes. If you think you are not dreaming, you just forget your dreams.

Most of our dreams are forgotten. **(fact)**

As much as 95% of all dreams are quickly forgotten shortly after waking. Within five minutes of waking, half of your dream is forgotten. Within ten minutes, 90% is gone.

Males and females dream differently. **(fact)**

In several studies, men were found to dream about weapons significantly more often than women did, while women dreamed about clothing more often than men.

Men's dreams usually contain more physical activity, while women's dreams contain more conversation. Women tend to have slightly longer dreams that feature more characters. Men dream about other men twice as often as they do about women, while women tend to dream about both men and women equally.

Animals don't dream. **(myth)**

Many of us think that when a sleeping dog wags its tail or moves its legs, it is dreaming. It is hard to say for sure, but researchers believe that animals do indeed dream. Studies have been done on many different animals, and they all show the same brain waves during dreaming sleep as humans.

Blind people can only dream in sounds. **(myth)**

Researchers have found that people who are blind from birth still seemed to experience pictures and images in their dreams, and they also had eye movements that we associate with visual dream recall. People who became blind after birth can see images in their dreams. People who are born blind see fewer visuals but have dreams involving emotion and their other senses of sound, smell, and touch.

Everyone's dreams are completely different. **(myth)**

Researchers have found that dreams have certain themes that are very common across many different people and cultures. For example, people from all over the world frequently dream about being chased, being attacked, or falling. Other common dream experiences include feeling frozen and unable to move, arriving late, flying, and being naked in public.

If you snore more, then you dream more. **(myth)**

Dreaming and snoring occur as separate activities more often than not. Snoring usually happens when we are in a deep sleep stage, though dreaming occurs at the REM stage, which is different and separate. Therefore, you are less likely to be dreaming if you are snoring.

Dreams can predict future health problems. **(fact)**

There is a rare sleep disorder that causes people to act out their dreams, sometimes with violent thrashes, kicks, and screams. Such violent dreams may be an early sign of brain disorders later in life, including Parkinson's disease and dementia, according to research published online on July 28, 2010, in the journal *Neurology*.

People who stay up late at night have more nightmares. **(fact)**

Research published in 2011 in the journal *Sleep and Biological Rhythms* revealed that night owls are more likely than those who go to bed early to experience nightmares. The researchers said the difference between going to bed late or early and the number of nightmares experienced was great, but they weren't sure what was causing the link.

All dreams are in colour. **(myth)**

Twelve per cent of people dream in black and white. In studies where dreamers have been awakened and asked to select colours from a chart that match those in their dreams, soft pastel colours are those most frequently chosen.

Dreams are mainly positive emotional experiences. **(myth)**

Over a period of more than 40 years, researcher Calvin S. Hall, PhD, collected over 50,000 dream accounts from college students. The dream accounts revealed that the most common emotions experienced in dreams are anxiety and negative emotions, which are, in general, much more common than positive ones.

You can't control your dreams. **(myth)**

A lucid dream is one where you know that you are dreaming even though you're still asleep. Many people have bad dreams or nightmares. These can happen over and over again. People can control these dreams and change the events in them to be less frightening. First, write down memories of the scary dream. After this think about how it might end differently.

It is dangerous if your muscles relax too much while you are dreaming. **(myth)**

During REM sleep many of our muscles relax completely, and this prevents us acting out our dreams. This is a normal and healthy reaction. If this system doesn't work properly, we may try to act out our dreams, especially if the dreams involve strong emotions.

Six years of your lifetime is spent dreaming. **(fact)**

On average a person can have anywhere between four and seven dreams a night.

Scientists are clear about the role of dreams. **(myth)**

Some scientists say we have dreams only because parts of our brain are stimulated when we are asleep, and they mean nothing. Others say dreams have value and importance. They say it is a kind of therapy for when we're feeling down. Having and remembering vivid dreams about stressful things in our lives may help deal with stress. Many people think that dreams contain messages, but the evidence for this is weak.

We mainly dream in pictures. **(fact)**

About two-thirds of dreams are mainly images, with fewer that involve sounds, movement, taste, or smell. It has been said that when we are awake we think in ideas, but when asleep we think in pictures.

Most dreams are totally random. **(myth)**

Dreams are often linked to real-life events from the past. Usually these are events or thoughts from one to two days before the dream.

Dreaming shuts our brains down. **(fact)**

When we are awake the front part of our brain controls how we make sense of the world. This shuts down during dreaming. Because of this, the dreaming brain puts together ideas that normally do not go together.

We only see faces we already know when we dream. **(fact)**

Our mind does not invent faces in our dreams. We see real faces of real people that we have seen during our life but may not know or remember. We have all seen hundreds of thousands of faces throughout our lives, so we have an endless supply of characters for our brain to use during our dreams.

Dreams help us solve puzzles. **(fact)**

Harvard psychologist Deirdre Barrett, who presented her theory in 2010 at the Association for Psychological Science meeting in Boston, has found that our sleeping hours may help us solve puzzles that have troubled us during the daytime hours.

According to Barrett, it's the visual and often illogical aspects of dreams that make them perfect for the creative and critical thinking that is necessary to solve some problems.

Less sleep means more intense dreams. **(fact)**

In a 2005 study published in *Sleep*, Nielsen showed that dream intensity increased with REM and sleep deprivation. People who were only getting about 25 minutes of REM sleep rated the quality of their dreams between 9 and 8 on a nine-point scale (1 being dull, 9 being dynamite).

Dream time capsule

Sometimes we dream about our future. We think about what we want to do, what our life will be like, or where we will live. Talk with your child about their dreams for the future. Ask them questions like the following, and then write down their answers or have them write down their answers or make drawings about them.

- What will you do when you are done with school? What job do you think you will have?
- Where do you want to live? What is it about that place that interests you?

- How do you think life will be different? For you? For the world?

- What hobbies do you think you will have? How will you spend your free time?

Put the responses in an envelope, label it or make a note on it to help you remember what is inside, and then store it somewhere that you are likely to find it when your child is older – when they are finishing school, moving out of the house, etc. It will be interesting at that time to see how much their dreams for the future have changed and have stayed the same.

Dreams of the people

Over time, leaders, musicians, and artists have talked about, sung about, and created art showing a common dream for humankind. Work with your child to find some examples. Here are a few examples that you can look for to get started:

- Lyrics from the song 'Imagine' by Beatle John Lennon

- Martin Luther King Jr.'s 'I Have a Dream' speech

- The Norman Rockwell painting *Rosie the Riveter*

Talk with your child about the messages being sent through these words and images. Work with your child to find other examples of people sharing their dreams about humankind through songs, speeches, or art. Discuss the following:

- Are there common themes or ideas that we see in the examples we have found?

- How might current events impact the dreams that people have for humankind?

- What are your dreams for humankind? How can you make a difference in making that happen?

Literature – all a dream?

The theme of dreaming is an important part of William Shakespeare's play *A Midsummer Night's Dream*. Almost every character in the play is asleep at some point, and this plays tricks on the reader or the audience, as we are made to wonder what is real and what is not real, what is awake time and what is dreaming.

Fairies, such as the naughty character Puck, play tricks on other characters throughout the night. Shakespeare has written it this way to tell us that dreams are playful, mischievous, and not easily understood. After a night of confusion the characters awaken not quite knowing what happened the night before but happy that they are back to some normality. Shakespeare is sending us the message that 'everything will be better in the morning' after a night of sleep and dreams.

At the end of the play Shakespeare plays an even bigger trick on the reader/audience. Find *A Midsummer Night's Dream*, act 4, scene 2, and read it with your child.

Through this famous speech, the mischievous Puck tells us that the whole play is a dream and the real sleepers were the readers or audience. Such a cool twist to the story, don't you think?

Try to create your own story which surprises the reader by revealing at the end that it was all a dream. Use the storyboard frame to help you.

Make sure you consider the following:

- How will you start your story?
- Who are the characters in it?
- What crazy, funny, or hard-to-believe things happen?
- How will you reveal that it was all a dream at the end?

Story board frame

Story Title

Main Character	Other Characters
Setting	**Key Events**

Story Beginning - Paragraph 1	Paragraph 2
Paragraph 3	**Paragraph 4**
Paragraph 5	**Ending**

The dreams of Pythagoras

Pythagoras is a very famous philosopher and mathematician. He lived about 2500 years ago and was born on the Greek island of Samos. From a very young age, Pythagoras was fascinated by mathematics. He spent his days thinking about numbers and their relationships and his nights dreaming about them.

Pythagoras believed numbers are all-powerful and everywhere. The world that we see, the sounds that we hear, and even the thoughts and emotions that go on in our minds are all made up of different numbers and their relationships to each other. He even produced a theory that translated the world of music into numbers.

Pythagoras dreamed that numbers were the answer to everything, and he began work proving this idea and developing laws of mathematics that we still use today.

One famous Pythagorean discovery was his theorem, which stated that

> *the square of the hypotenuse of a right-angled triangle is equal to the sum of the squares of the other two sides.*

Sound complicated? It's really not if you think about it. Here it is explained in easy steps.

1. We need a right-angled triangle. This is a triangle with two sides that meet to form a 90-degree angle or 'right angle'. A corner of a square or rectangle is also an example of a right angle.

2. In a right-angled triangle, the **hypotenuse** is the side directly across from the right angle. It is the only side of the triangle that is not a part of the right angle. On the diagram, the hypotenuse is green.

3. If we call the sides of our triangle a, b, and c, then Pythagoras tells us that if we know the length of a and b, we can work out the length of c.

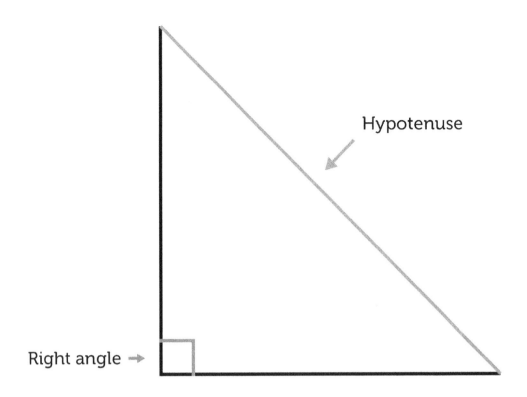

Right Triangle

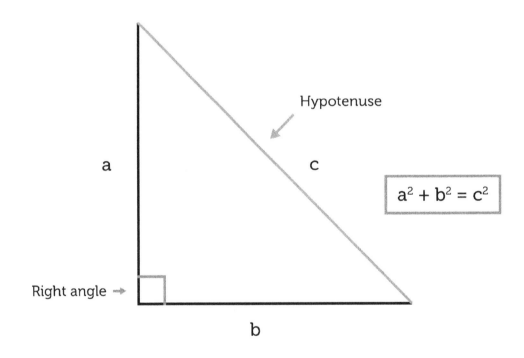

$$a^2 + b^2 = c^2$$

 Lessons to support learning

Pythagorean theorem applied

We can show how this works with building bricks. If we make a square along each side of a right-angled triangle, the square on the longest side uses the same number of bricks as the other two sides' squares put together.

- We used 2 x 2 sized LEGO bricks.

- We drew a triangle with sides which were 3 cm long, 4 cm long, and 5 cm long (three bricks long, four bricks long, and five bricks long).

- We lined the bricks against the sides of our triangle.

- We continued to form the bricks into squares (e.g., 3 x 3, 4 x 4, 5 x 5)

- When we counted all the bricks up, we can prove that Pythagoras was correct: 9 bricks + 16 bricks = 25 bricks.

ChallengingLEARNING   Lessons to support learning

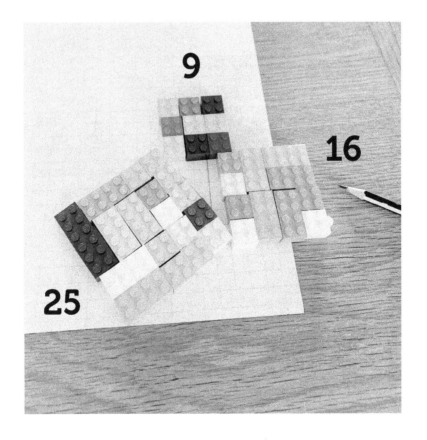

ChallengingLEARNING | Lessons to support learning

Try proving Pythagoras's theorem yourself with building bricks. Create your own right-angled triangles to test the theorem out.

Here are some ways that Pythagoras's dream about the relationship of numbers which led to his famous theorem helps us in our everyday lives. We can use this theorem to

- determine how long a ladder needs to be to reach an upstairs window in a house;
- work out the materials needed to construct a roof for a house;
- work out the shortest distance between two points we are travelling between.

Malala and her dream – Mystery

Can you solve this Mystery and answer the question *Was Malala right to fight for her dream*? Explore the following cards to build an answer to this question.

Malala Yousafzai from Pakistan always dreamed of going to school, getting a good education, and then getting a great job. This was not only her dream for herself but her dream for ALL children around the world. When the Taliban regime came to power in Malala's region of Pakistan, they destroyed schools and made it illegal for girls to attend classes. This made Malala even more determined to fight to make her dream a reality.

Cut up all the information cards and mix them up before sorting through the evidence. Consider the following:

- Which way could you sort the information to make it easier to process and consider? Here are some examples:

  Pros/Cons, World impact / Personal impact, Important information / Not important information, Safe/Dangerous, Worthwhile / Not worthwhile, etc.

- Are any of the information cards irrelevant or not needed?
- Are any of the information cards the key to answering the question?

Malala Yousafzai was born July 12, 1997

The Taliban were known around the world for their bad treatment of women.

The BBC published translations of her writings about her life under Taliban rule.

The Taliban said girls could no longer go to school.

12th July It has since been named "Malala Day".

David Trumble, an award-winning artist, made a cartoon of Malala as a Disney princess

She was outspoken against the Taliban, stating, "How dare the Taliban take away my basic right to education?" Her speech was covered by newspapers and TV channels.

In 2009, at age 11, Malala wrote a blog about her life in Pakistan.

Malala Yousafzai had a dream that education and schooling should be available for all children across the world, girls as well as boys.

Mulala is originally from the town of Mingora in the Swat District.

Mulala's father, Ziauddin Yousafzai, was determined to give her every opportunity a boy would have.

The Taliban is an Islamic militant group working in Afghanistan and Pakistan

Lessons to support learning

Malala's book was banned in Pakistani private schools.

The Taliban have said that they still want to murder Mulala.

She had two five-hour long operations on 2 February 2013. She had a titanium plate put over the hole in her skull and a cochlear implant fitted so she could hear again.

In October 2013 Mulala met President Obama, Michelle Obama, and their daughter Malia in the Oval Office.

Having a baby girl is not always cause for celebration in Pakistan.

Parents who refuse to send their children to school and employers who hire school-aged children can be imprisoned under the new Right to Education Bill law in Pakistan.

In October 2013 a book about her life *I am Malala: The Girl Who Stood Up for Education and Was Shot* by the Taliban was published, with her help

On 12 July 2013, at age 16, she made a speech at headquarters of the United Nations, stressing the right to education for all and saying: "the pen is mightier than the sword".

Mulala's father was a teacher and ran a girls' school in their village.

Malala's blog was called *Diary of a Pakistani Schoolgirl*. Malala wrote under the pen name "Gul Makai", a heroine from a Pashtun folktale

Malala spoke out publicly on behalf of girls and their right to learn. And this made her a target.

Malala loved school. But everything changed when the Taliban took control of our town in Swat Valley.

In October 2012, on her way home from school, a masked gunman boarded her school bus and asked, "Who is Malala?" He shot her on the left side of her head.

After months of surgeries and rehabilitation, she joined her family in her new home in the U.K.

She was determined to continue to fight for her dream until every girl could go to school.

She travels to many countries to meet girls fighting poverty, wars, child marriage and gender discrimination in order to go to school.

She established Malala Fund, a charity dedicated to giving every girl an opportunity to achieve a future she chooses.

In recognition of her work fighting for her dream, she received the Nobel Peace Prize in December 2014 and became the youngest-ever Nobel laureate.

Challenging LEARNING   Lessons to support learning

Malala always dreamed of a rich education so that she could become a teacher, a doctor or a politician when she was older.

Every day she fights for her dream to ensure all girls receive 12 years of free, safe, quality education.

Her early childhood was one of happiness and peace and love.

Her father taught her that she could achieve anything she worked hard for.

When Malala was ten years old, the Taliban began to take over the region where she lived.

The Taliban said that women were to stay at home.

Despite being worried about the safety of his family, Malala's father agreed to let Malala write a blog for the BBC.

The Taliban said that if a woman left her home, she was to wear a burqa (a garment that covers the body, head, and face) and she must be accompanied by a male relative.

The Taliban demanded that girls' schools had to be shut down. Girls' schools that were not shut down were burned or destroyed.

Malala's blog was called *Diary of a Pakistani Schoolgirl*. Malala wrote under the pen name "Gul Makai", a heroine from a Pashtun folktale.

The Taliban made laws stating that women were not allowed to vote or to have jobs.

Malala soon became famous for writing her blog. She also began to speak in public about the treatment of the Taliban

Eventually, the Pakistani government took back control of the area and Malala was able to return to school.

The Taliban were very angry with Malala.

Malala was warned to stop speaking out and received death threats.

Getting shot didn't stop Malala. On her sixteenth birthday Malala gave a speech to the United Nations

In her speech to the UN, Malala again spoke about her dream of wanting all girls to get an education.

She didn't want revenge or violence on the Taliban (even the man who shot her), she just wanted peace and educational opportunities for all. Girls and boys.

Challenging LEARNING | Lessons to support learning

Mulala has two younger brothers.

Malala was warned to stop speaking out and received death threats

Young people now have voice among world education leaders thanks to Malala.

The UN speech on Malala's 16th birthday, brought together more than 600 young leaders from around the world in support of universal education for all children.

The Malala petition led to the success of Pakistan passing the Right to Education Bill 2012, guaranteeing that ALL children, aged between five and 16, have access to free education.

The UN made a new pledge to aim for children everywhere, boys and girls alike, to be able to complete a full course of primary schooling by 2015.

When she turned 18 in 2015, she was still pushing for her dream of 'education for all'. She called on world leaders to "invest in books, not bullets."

At 11 years old, Malala began talking about her dream for girls to have access to education.

Death threats made against Mulala were published in the newspaper and written on Facebook.

Questions to consider:

- What do you think you would have done in Malala's position?

- Do you think Malala was right to risk her life and the safety of her family to speak out about her views?

- Why do you think it was so important to Malala that her voice was heard? Do you think Malala has now achieved her dream?

- Should we all follow Malala's lead and have big dreams for changing the world? Do you think Malala's struggle was worth it?

- What do you think Malala's life would be like now if she hadn't stood up for what she believed in?

- Do you think Malala was courageous to speak up for herself and for the education of 60 million girls around the world? Has she inspired you to speak out about anything?

Are your dreams realistic?

We all dream about things we want – places we want to go, items we want to buy, or gifts that we want to give. Sometimes our dreams are realistic and can be achieved in the short term, but sometimes they are more out of reach and require planning and saving. Talk with your child about a dream 'want' that they have. It could be a new pet, a vacation, a gift for a family member, a shopping spree in the city, or a new gaming system. Whatever it is, talk about everything that would be needed for their dream 'want'. For example, if it is a vacation, include travel, food, hotel, fees for activities, etc.

Help your child to research the costs and complete a budget sheet similar to the following example for purchasing a dog:

General description	Product/Service to purchase	Cost
Buying the dog	From the local rescue/humane society	$300
Food	25 lb. bags of food ($20 per month x 12)	$240
	Treats – bones, training treats, etc. ($10 per month x 12)	$120
Vet bills	Shots, pills, registration, etc.	$300
Supplies	Toys	$50
	Leash/Collar	$20
	Dog bed	$30
	Crate	$50
	Total cost for the first year	$1,110

As you complete the budget, use questions like the following to discuss:

- How can we find out all of the costs that might be associated with your dream? Are there other ways to get this information?

- What if something comes up that we didn't account for? How can we plan for that?

- What surprised you the most as you researched the cost of your dream?

- How realistic is it that you can achieve this dream this year? In five years? Ever? How do you know?

- How much would you have to save per week/month in order to save what you need? How might you do that?

Aboriginal Dreamtime

In Australian Aboriginal culture, life is based on strongly held beliefs which are called the **Dreamtime** or the **Dreaming**.

The **Dreamtime** is at the centre of all Aboriginal culture. It explains where the Aboriginal people and culture came from and how the culture developed. Most Aboriginal people believe that all life today (human, animal, or plant) can be traced directly back to the great spirit ancestors of the Dreamtime.

The Aboriginal people believe that everything that happens leaves a record of itself in the land. Everything in nature is a result of the actions of the spiritual beings who created the world. The meaning and importance of particular places and creatures is linked to their origin in the Dreamtime, and certain places have a particular power, which the Aborigines call its *dreaming*. In this dreaming lies the pureness and sacredness of the Earth.

There are many Aboriginal Dreamtime (creation) stories which help us to understand Aboriginal culture and beliefs better. Dreamtime stories often explain how the country, animals, and people came to be as they are. They tell us when things were made, why they were made, and how they were made. 'The Rainbow Serpent' is one example of a Dreamtime story. There are many versions of 'The Rainbow Serpent' online that you can read with your child.

The Aboriginal peoples have a great history of recreating these stories through artwork. Did you know that an Aboriginal artist cannot paint a story that does not belong to them through family? They inherit the rights to these stories which are passed down through generations of their family.

Create your own Aboriginal Dreamtime story art

- Research Aboriginal symbols that are used in storytelling and artworks. Some of these symbols may include animals and their tracks, tools (e.g., spears, boomerangs, etc.), natural elements (e.g., waterholes and sand hills), or people.

- Collect some stones or pebbles that are a good shape to draw or paint on.

- Using markers or paint, your fingers, brushes, cotton buds, and/or sticks to dip in the paint, draw a symbol on each stone to represent different parts of your story.

- You can recreate the story 'The Rainbow Serpent' or another traditional Dreamtime story of your choice.

- Research the significance of the colours used in Aboriginal art (white, yellow, red, and black are commonly used colours) and some of the traditional techniques and styles they use (e.g., dot painting and cross-hatch).

Bad dreams and dream catchers

Talk to your child about dreams and recall times when they have had bad dreams that have woken them up with fears or worries. Share with them the following information about how a Native American tribe, the Ojibwe tribe, believes they can protect their young from bad dreams:

The Ojibwe tribe creates 'dream catchers' that are like spider webs that will capture any harmful dreams before reaching the child. They believe these dream catchers, which are designed to look like spider webs with beads and feathers as decoration, will trap bad dreams while letting good dreams escape through the holes in the web.

They place the dream catchers above beds or sleeping areas so that anyone sleeping there will be protected from bad dreams and dark spirits.

Work with your child to design and create a unique dream catcher.

- Use a wooden ring, or create a square, hexagon, or octagon by gluing popsicle sticks together.

- Use coloured yarn or string and wrap it around a spot on the ring or polygon figure, then run the yarn across the open space and wrap it on that side. Keep repeating until you have a web.

- You can decorate the web in different ways: you can run beads onto the string as you are creating the web; you can glue objects like feathers, beads, pictures, etc. to the web after it is complete; or you can attach feathers, beads, pictures, buttons, etc. to the outside of the dream catcher.

Talk with your child about ways to make it unique and special to them:

- Use their favourite colours.
- Include pictures or items that will 'attract' things that they like so that they guide their dreams.
- Put pictures of family that will 'protect' them while they sleep.

LESSON 4 BIG QUESTION – WHAT IS SUCCESS?

Idea One:
Being successful makes you popular and well liked

Idea Two:
People can be jealous and resentful of other people's success

Success

STRONGER LEARNING
for STRONGER LIVES

Dinner table conversations

Concept: Success

Main question: What is success?

Follow-up questions:

- What is the difference between success and fame?
- Is it possible to define success?
- Would one universal definition of success work for every person and every situation?
- Can you be accomplished and not successful?
- What is the difference between winning and succeeding?

- What is the connection between success and perfection?

- Is success simply the opposite to failure?

Concept: Success

Main question: Are there different types of success?

Follow-up questions:

- Can anybody be successful?

- Is it impossible not to be successful at some point in your life?

- How different does success look for different people?

- Could failure ever be perceived as a less recognised form of success?

- How closely is success defined by our individual core values?

- How much is success dependent on reputation?

- If you are happy and/or healthy, does that mean you are successful?

- What is the ultimate goal of success?

Concept: Success

Main question: Is success dependent on failure?

Follow-up questions:

- How much is risk-taking an essential part of being successful?

- Do we have to completely master something to be seen as a success at it?

- If we fail at something does that always mean that we are unsuccessful?

- How many times can you fail and still be regarded as a success?

- To what extent is success based on achievement against adversity?

- Do you have to feel proud of your achievements to be successful?

- Can you be successful yet feel ashamed of your actions?

Concept: Success

Main question: Is success really achievable?

Follow-up questions:

- To what degree is success a continuous journey?

- Can success be measured?

- How much is our success dependent upon our perspective of what is successful?

- What might the secret to success be?

- To what degree is success an idealistic quest to 'have it all'?

- Is success always something you can earn?

- If you don't feel good about your success, are you actually unsuccessful?

- In order to be a successful artist, would every piece of art you produce have to be a success?

- How many pieces of your art would have to be unsuccessful before you were regarded as a failure?

Maths game – hit the target

In this maths game, success is determined by how close you can come to the target. You can add additional success criteria (like using two different operations) as you play. You need a deck of cards and at least two people to play.

- Turn over the top card. This is the target number.

- Each player then draws three cards from the deck and arranges all three cards into a number sentence. For example, if the target is 4 and the three cards are 10, 5, and 4, you may create the number sentence 10 / 5 = 2 + 4 = 6.

- Whoever gets the closest to 4 keeps all of the cards (including the target card). If there is a tie, the cards go back into a discard pile which can be shuffled and used when the cards in the centre run out.

Success criteria

When completing a task, aspiring to make a change, or setting goals, it is a good idea to establish success criteria. This can even be important when just asking your child to complete chores at home.

Practice establishing success criteria with your child. Success criteria describe what success looks like. They answer questions like these: 'How do you know you are good at . . . ?' 'How do you know you have succeeded with . . . ?' 'What does success look like in . . . ?' Choose a goal or a task and decide what the success criteria will be. Use guiding questions like these:

- What do we want to see, feel, or experience at the end?

- How do we know we have accomplished our goal?

Successful estimation

We make estimations in many different situations for various purposes. Depending on the situation, our estimates will vary in how accurate or how close to the actual answer they are. In some instances, there is not one specific answer, only estimates.

Talk with your child about how to determine the success of an estimate. What makes for a successful estimate? Is it close? Realistic? Useful? Establish success criteria for a good estimate. Once you have success criteria established, talk about estimates for the following:

- Weight of a banana

- Height of the largest pyramid in Egypt

- Number of stones in the pyramid

- Number of words in a *Harry Potter* book

- Number of miles across Australia

- Age of a dinosaur fossil or bone

- Weight of the Eiffel Tower

Discuss how you might go about finding the estimates and challenge your child to make an estimate.

After coming up with the estimates, talk about how well you met the success criteria and whether or not you would change any of the estimates.

Talk about estimates we make in real life and how they might be useful to some jobs.

What is the difference between being famous and being successful?

Everyone knows your name	Being rich	Demonstrating determination
Accomplishing your goals	Having the respect of others	Working hard
Showing motivation	Having a positive impact on the world	Lots of followers on social media
Inspiring others to do something	Influencing change	Having good looks
Demonstrating strong leadership	Being emulated by others	Being listened to by others
Being a source of authority	Being featured on television	Being featured in magazines

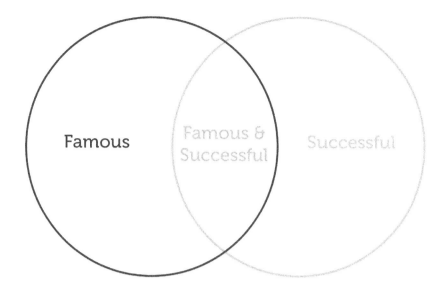

Use the listed characteristics and the Venn diagram template to compare the similarities and differences between being famous and being successful. You can cut each characteristic out and your child/ren can place them in the part of the diagram that they think they should go into. If there are any characteristics that do not apply to being famous or successful, they should go outside of the diagram.

Challenge your child's thinking and reasoning as they make their choices.

- Would that always make someone famous?
- Can you think of someone who is famous, but not very successful?
- Can you be famous for doing bad things? Can you become successful by doing bad things?
- Is it possible to be emulated by others without being listened to?
- Is it possible to be featured on television without being famous or successful?

Ranking success indicators

Refer to the strategy guide for information about diamond ranking.

Talk to your child about what makes someone successful and what attributes most contribute to success. Brainstorm some indicators of success. Then cut out the following cards (and add any that you have come up with) and have your child arrange them into a diamond four (for younger children) or a diamond nine, placing the concept most important for success at the top and the one least important for success at the bottom. Since they will not use all of the cards, you can repeat the process by eliminating some cards or choosing some cards that must be used.

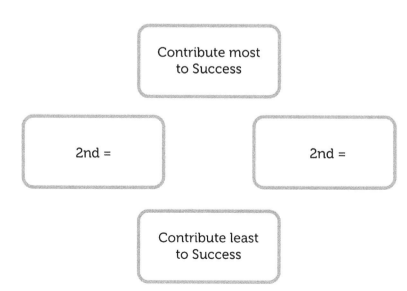

```
                    ┌─────────────────┐
                    │  Contribute most │
                    │   to Success     │
                    └─────────────────┘

        ┌─────────────┐           ┌─────────────┐
        │     2=      │           │     2=      │
        └─────────────┘           └─────────────┘

 ┌─────────────┐   ┌─────────────┐   ┌─────────────┐
 │     3=      │   │     3=      │   │     3=      │
 └─────────────┘   └─────────────┘   └─────────────┘

        ┌─────────────┐           ┌─────────────┐
        │     4=      │           │     4=      │
        └─────────────┘           └─────────────┘

                    ┌─────────────────┐
                    │ Contribute least │
                    │   to Success     │
                    └─────────────────┘
```

Number of friends	Amount of money	Influence/Power	Intelligence	Leadership
Fame	Strength	Wisdom	Honesty	Education
Kindness	Effort	Confidence	Vision	Courage
Resilience	Responsibility	Commitment	Healthy lifestyle	Ambition

Storybook success surpass

Cut the cards apart, shuffle them, and place them in the middle of the playing surface. This game is for two people, and the youngest person in the game will go first. On each turn, follow these steps:

- Both players draw one card.

- The person whose turn it is will look at their card and decide which of their success indicator ratings will beat their partner's card. They will then call out that success characteristic.

- Both partners lay down their card and whoever has the highest score for that indicator keeps both cards.

- If both cards have the same rating, both cards go to the bottom of the pile of unused cards.

- The game is complete when there are no more cards to be drawn. The winner is the player with the most cards.

Big Bad Wolf

Fame - 7
Friendly - 0
Bravery - 5
Wisdom - 3
Strength - 9
Honesty - 2

©2020 www.challenginglearning.com

Three Little Pigs

Fame - 6
Friendly - 6
Bravery - 1
Wisdom - 2
Strength - 3
Honesty - 8

©2020 www.challenginglearning.com

Goldilocks

Fame - 4
Friendly - 5
Bravery - 4
Wisdom - 3
Strength - 2
Honesty - 1

©2020 www.challenginglearning.com

Hansel and Gretel

Fame - 2
Friendly - 4
Bravery - 3
Wisdom - 2
Strength - 3
Honesty - 5

©2020 www.challenginglearning.com

Harry Potter

Fame - 10
Friendly - 8
Bravery - 8
Wisdom - 4
Strength - 3
Honesty - 2

©2020 www.challenginglearning.com

Gandalf

Fame - 3
Friendly - 6
Bravery - 9
Wisdom - 9
Strength - 9
Honesty - 9

©2020 www.challenginglearning.com

The Grinch

Fame - 8
Friendly - 1
Bravery - 2
Wisdom - 4
Strength - 6
Honesty - 2

Rudolph

Fame - 7
Friendly - 9
Bravery - 7
Wisdom - 3
Strength - 7
Honesty - 6

The Lion from Wizard of Oz

Fame - 3
Friendly - 9
Bravery - 0
Wisdom - 2
Strength - 6
Honesty - 8

Peter Pan

Fame - 7
Friendly - 6
Bravery - 10
Wisdom - 5
Strength - 8
Honesty - 4

Eeyore

Fame - 3
Friendly - 6
Bravery - 1
Wisdom - 7
Strength - 4
Honesty - 10

Aladdin

Fame - 9
Friendly - 6
Bravery - 8
Wisdom - 2
Strength - 6
Honesty - 0

Peter Rabbit

Fame - 5
Friendly - 8
Bravery - 7
Wisdom - 3
Strength - 2
Honesty - 1

Pippi Longstocking

Fame - 2
Friendly - 7
Bravery - 8
Wisdom - 8
Strength - 10
Honesty - 2

Matilda

Fame - 2
Friendly - 6
Bravery - 9
Wisdom - 10
Strength - 4
Honesty - 7

Humpty Dumpty

Fame - 4
Friendly - 7
Bravery - 2
Wisdom - 0
Strength - 0
Honesty - 5

Little Red Hen

Fame - 1
Friendly - 4
Bravery - 6
Wisdom - 9
Strength - 8
Honesty - 8

Gingerbread Man

Fame - 4
Friendly - 2
Bravery - 4
Wisdom - 3
Strength - 1
Honesty - 2

Mary Poppins

Fame - 8
Friendly - 10
Bravery - 6
Wisdom - 8
Strength - 5
Honesty - 9

Pinocchio

Fame - 6
Friendly - 3
Bravery - 2
Wisdom - 2
Strength - 1
Honesty - 1

Ladder to success or steps to success

Share the story of JK Rowling – from living in poverty to becoming the first female billionaire author. Her success was definitely not overnight or easy. There were many steps along the way that led her to her success and fortune. Talk about the following steps and how they were a part of her ultimate success.

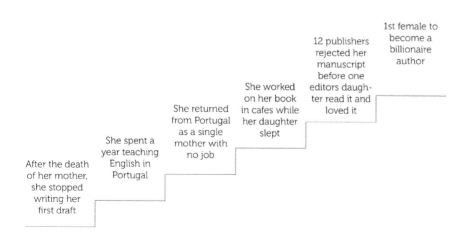

After the death of her mother, she stopped writing her first draft

She spent a year teaching English in Portugal

She returned from Portugal as a single mother with no job

She worked on her book in cafes while her daughter slept

12 publishers rejected her manuscript before one editors daughter read it and loved it

1st female to become a billionaire author

Have your child identify a success they would like to experience. Talk about all of the smaller steps/successes they will need to achieve along the way. Create a ladder or stairs to show their aspired journey. Use the following questions to guide the thinking and planning (sample goal of running a mile in parentheses):

- What needs to happen in order for you to reach your goal? (I need to be fit enough and strong enough to run continuously for the length of one mile.)

- Where are you now? What have you done so far or what can you do at this point? (I can run continuously for two minutes.)

- What do you need to do to get from where you are to achieving your goal? (I need to extend the time that I run a little bit each time I run. I need to run regularly. I need to stick with it until I get to a mile.)

Four corners – what contributes to success?

Usain Bolt, a Jamaican sprinter, is a legend in the sport of track and field. He has had a tremendous amount of success in the sport and has worked hard to achieve it. Use this activity to explore with your child/ren the biggest contributors to his success. Cut apart and read through the following cards containing quotes from and information about Usain Bolt with your child/ren. Introduce the terms 'beliefs/vision', 'skill', 'luck/opportunity', and 'effort'. Talk about what each one means and how they contribute to success.

Using the following opinion corners frame, encourage your child/ren to place the cards in the corner where the statement best fits. They should place each quote in the correct corner on the opinion corners frame and give their reasons for their choices as well as their opinions about how the quote or statement describes that contribution to success.

Challenge their reasons and thinking by asking questions like these:

- Does this refer to his personal beliefs/vision for his success, or about opportunities he has had?

- How is opportunity different from skill?

- At what point do you think Usain considered himself a success?

- How do you define Usain's success? Does it relate more to his gold medals or his perseverance?

"I train for 11 months of the year, six days a week."

- Usain Bolt

"It's hard work, sweat and sacrifice. I've sacrificed so much throughout the season, throughout the years. I've been through so much."

- Usain Bolt

"Well, my single greatest goal is to become the greatest, pretty much. That's what I work towards. I want to be remembered as a great sportsman, to have a place in history."

- Usain Bolt

"Training gives you confidence and this helps your state of mind. I know if I'm in good shape it's going to be very hard to beat me, this confidence is very important in performing well.

– Usain Bolt

He is a Jamaican born athletic sprinter, and was born on 21st August 1986 in Trelawny, Jamaica.

"World juniors made me who I am today...It was one of the toughest races of my life up to this day. I was so nervous running in front of my home crowd."

– Usain Bolt

"You could see this tall young boy – just raw natural talent," remembers Lorna Thorpe, who was then head of sport at the school where Usain Bolt was a student.

Bolt wasn't particularly interested in sprinting. He loved playing football and cricket.

Usain Bolt stated, "there was still room for improvement," even though he won the 100m at the Olympic Stadium in 2013.

"I've proven that I'm the greatest in this sport and, for me, it's mission accomplished."

– Usain Bolt

Bolt made his Olympic debut as a 17-year-old at Athens 2004, where he went out in the opening round of the 200m because of a hamstring injury.

Jamaica (with a population of just 3 million) has won 14 Olympic gold medals, with many of them in sprinting.

"He has lots of fast twitch muscle fibres that can respond quickly, coupled with his vast stride is what gives him such an extraordinary fast time."

-John Barrow
Cambridge University

By the age of twelve, Bolt had become the school's fastest runner over the 100 metres distance.

Bolt became the first man in history to defend both the 100 m and 200 m Olympic sprint titles.

As a child he played football and cricket with his brother.

"I'm confident that I'm going to win, but I never think, 'No one can beat me.'"

- Usain Bolt

Bolt became the first man in history to defend both the 100 m and 200 m Olympic sprint titles.

Bolt paid over £10,000 to adopt an abandoned cheetah cub - named Lightning Bolt - in Nairobi, and continues to pay £2,300 a year to pay for its upkeep at the orphanage.

Bolt owns a restaurant in Jamaica.

"I wouldn't say I'm a phenomenon, just a great athlete."

- Usain Bolt

"There you go. I'm the greatest." Jamaican sprinter Usain Bolt speaking after his "triple triple" of golds in the 100m, 200m and 4x100m relays.

"You have to find that one thing that you know is going to motivate you. You might not enjoy training for example but you have to love competing and winning."

- Usain Bolt

Bolt's height is 6 feet 5 inches whereas his competitors tend to be 6ft 2 inches and lower.

"If I start like that in the world championships I will probably finish fifth. I need to work with my coach and figure out how to be more explosive out of the blocks and not so slow."

- Usain Bolt reflecting after one of his races in 2013.

He became the youngest gold medallist at the Junior World Championships when he was only 15 years old.

In 2009, Bolt became the world record holder in both the 100m (9.58 secs) and the 200m (19.19 secs) races.

"He has lots of fast twitch muscle fibres that can respond quickly, coupled with his vast stride is what gives him such an extraordinary fast time."

- John Barrow Cambridge University

By the age of twelve, Bolt had become the school's fastest runner over the 100 metres distance.

Bolt became the first man in history to defend both the 100 m and 200 m Olympic sprint titles.

Opinion corners frame

Beliefs/ Vision	Luck/ Opportunity
Effort	Skill

Sarah's wallpapering project

Sarah is planning to wallpaper her room, but she has a limited budget. She needs to carefully plan her budget so that she does not run out of money before wallpapering the room. Use the following activities to judge what will lead to her success.

What is the most important thing Sarah needs to do to make sure her wallpapering project is a success? Choose nine of the following cards (see the following table) and rank them with the most important action or criterion for success at the top and the least important at the bottom.

Match patterns up carefully	Know how to subtract different amounts of money	Tidy up after herself
Choose the right colour of wallpaper	Know how to calculate volume	Know how to calculate area
Use a tape measure accurately	Work out the height of the room	Work out the width of the room
Know the length of the room	Calculate the weight of the doors and windows	Know the dimensions of the doors and windows
Find out how wide the wallpaper is	Find out how long a roll of wallpaper is	Add money together accurately
Multiply different amounts of money together	Know how to make a good cup of tea	Understand what her budget is

- What is the most important thing she needs to know or do to make this project a success?
- What do you think is the least important factor for the success of her project?

Introduce the following information and support your child/ren to re-rank the cards again, keeping in mind the new information they have available to them.

Sarah has a budget of £300.

Her room is 6 x 4 m. The ceiling is 2 ½ m high.

There are two windows and two doors into the lounge with a combined area of 7 m^2.

Rolls of wallpaper are 50 cm wide and just under 8 m long. – You can only use whole lengths of paper on a wall (no horizontal joints).

There are four choices of wallpaper:

budget quality – £10 per roll

standard quality – £15 per roll

high quality – £20 per roll

luxury   – £25 per roll

- Is there any difference between your first and second rankings? What has changed?
- What was the most important mathematics skill Sarah (you) would have to use to make this project a success?
- What other projects could she apply the same thinking to?
- What would she need to know if she was going to buy a pot of paint to decorate the room instead of wallpaper?
- How many rolls of wallpaper does Sarah need?
- What is the best quality she can afford?
- What do you think Sarah's ultimate aim or goal is for this project? For example:

  To decorate the room for the least amount of money

  To get the best quality of decoration for her budget

  To achieve the most professional look for the room décor

  To make the room look pretty

  To decorate the room in the easiest way possible

  To decorate the room in the quickest way possible

  To have fun while decorating the room

- How does the 'goal' or aim of the project affect the criteria for success you choose?
- Would the most important factor for success be different if the aim was to 'make the room pretty' rather than 'decorate it for the least amount of money'?
- Try ranking the cards for each different goal and see if they differ or stay the same in their rank of importance.

3. LESSONS ABOUT OUR LIVES

LESSON 5 BIG QUESTION – WHAT IS COST?

Idea One:
We should always work out the cost of something before we buy it.

Idea Two:
We should treat ourselves once in a while as we are worth it.

Cost?

STRONGER LEARNING
for STRONGER LIVES

Dinner table conversations

Concept: Cost

Main question: What is cost?

Follow-up questions:

- What is the difference between cost and price?
- How do you know what something costs?
- What affects the cost of something?
- Is cost always measured using money?
- How many different kinds of cost are there?
- Can personal cost be shared with others?
- Who decides the cost of something?

Concept: Cost

Main question: How important is cost?

Follow-up questions:
- What happens when something costs more than you can afford?
- If you spend more money on a gift, does that mean you care more?

- How does the cost of an item affect our choices?
- Is personal cost more important than monetary cost?
- How important would something need to be for cost not to matter?
- How might being able to buy things that cost a lot make you powerful?

Concept: Cost

Main question: Does everything have a cost?

Follow-up questions:

- Do costs always have a price?
- If something is 'priceless', does that mean it doesn't have a cost?
- When is there a cost for our behaviour and actions?
- What is the cost of climate change?
- What is the cost of not completing your homework?
- What are the costs of never reading a book?
- What makes something expensive?
- Do you only get what you pay for?
- What are the costs of never taking risks?

Concept: Cost

Main question: How can we best manage cost?

Follow-up questions:

- What might be the risks of doing something without knowing the costs?
- If you pay more do you always get more?
- What happens if we always spend more money than we have?
- How much does the cost of something influence your desire to have it?
- When might it be okay for other people to cover your costs for things?
- Are there benefits to all costs?
- How can we be sure if something is worth the cost or not?
- Are sale or promotional items always more cost effective than non-sale or non-promotional items?

Picture book activity

Alexander, Who Used to Be Rich Last Sunday by Judith Viorst is a good book to begin discussing the concept of cost.

It can be found in a bookstore, a library, or online. Here is a YouTube version: www.youtube.com/watch?v=dXNBUhYkRRI.

Here are a few activities/questions to go along with the story:

- Calculate how much money each of his siblings has.
- Add up the money that Alexander spends as the story progresses.
- Ask your child what they would do with a dollar. What could they buy? Would they save it? Why?
- Do you think we should have fines in our house for poor choices? What would they be?
- What would you say to Alexander if he asked for your help to save his money?

Cost memory game

Use the memory game cards attached to this activity pack to play this game.

- Cut out all of the cards and lay them face down on a table in a grid pattern – four rows and five columns.
- Take turns turning two cards over.
- If the two cards match in that one is an object and the other one is a reasonable price for that object, you may keep the cards. Otherwise, turn them back over.
- Keep taking turns until all of the cards have been paired up. Whoever has the most cards wins.

Lollipop	New Car	$1/£1	$15,000/ £12,000
Pet Dog	New House	$300/£240	$150,000/ £120,000
Book	Pizza	$15/£12	$15/£12
Shoes	Ice Cream Cone	$50/£40	$1/£1
Computer	Gaming System	$600/£400	$300/£240

Cost of wishes

Ask your child/ren to think about something that they are really wishing for. It could be a dog, a cat, a fish tank, or maybe it is a vacation to Disney World. Whatever it is, have a discussion about all of the costs that would be involved and then research them together (or, for older children, encourage them to do their own research) to find out what the total cost would be.

Have your child write up a plan for his/her commitments to help with the cost. It might be that they will help to raise money (and provide examples of how they will do this), or maybe they will commit to reducing costs in other areas.

Ask your child to present their plan to you using pictures, graphs, or other visuals along with a verbal presentation.

Game – quick spend

The goal of this game is to quickly pick out a specified number of items from a catalogue, a sale flyer, or a website with items for sale. You can change the number of items or the goal amount to spend to vary the game.

Here is an example:

- Using a sale flyer, each person has 90 seconds to pick out five items.

- Make note of the prices – write them down, circle them, star them, etc. – but you can't write them down and add them.

- At the end of 90 seconds, add everyone's five items, and whoever is the closest to £50 or $50 wins that round.

Opportunity cost

This is a term used in economics, and it means the cost of something in terms of lost opportunity. For example, if your town decides to build a new office building on an open piece of land, the opportunity cost is the OTHER ways the land could have been used. For example, it could have been made into a park where children can play, or it could have been made into a restaurant.

Use this idea of **opportunity cost** this week as you decide how to spend your time. When you have a choice, talk about all of the options and weigh the positives of each to ensure that you are getting most out of your time. Ask questions like these:

- Will this option allow us to do something together?

- Which option allows us to do something we haven't done for a while?

- Should we consider the weather for today before we decide?

- If we decide not to do _____, what is something good that might happen? What is something that we might miss out on?

A priceless poster

Does everything have a cost or price? Can everything be bought?

Is there anything you can think of that is so special, so unique, so important to you that no matter how much money you were offered for it, you would not be tempted to sell it? We talk about these kinds of things as being 'priceless'.

This could be a photograph, a memory, a pet, a relationship, an object you own, a special teddy from being a baby, an award or certificate you earned, a family heirloom, or anything else that is so important to you that you could never replace it and so would never want to lose it.

Support your child/ren to create a poster advertising this special thing. They can put a photograph of it on the poster or do a drawing of it. They can explain what makes it 'priceless' to them, label it with words to show how it makes them feel, and highlight the things that are particularly special about it.

ChallengingLEARNING | Lessons to support learning

Money grab

Fill a bag or a bowl with a variety of coins. Have your child close his/her eyes and grab a handful of coins out of the bag. Next, you grab a handful of coins. Place your handfuls on the table and look at them. Estimate who has more money in their pile, then count them to see. Ask questions like the following:

- Does more coins always equate to more money?
- What makes it hard to estimate when looking at the pile of coins?
- What if we only had coins to pay for things? How would that be different?

Cost challenge

There are many important things that make our lives better or worse depending on whether we have them or not. Do we need some of these more than others? Does that make some worth more than others? How do you decide which qualities are worth the most and which qualities are worth the least? How would apply a cost to these?

Imagine you are a market seller who is selling all these 'qualities for a good life' at your stall. You have 20 price tags (one for each quality), and you have to decide how you will price each one at your stall. You can only use each price tag once. Use the cards that follow or create your own.

- Which quality do you think should be priced at £1 million / $1 million?
- Which one should only cost the buyer 1 p / 1 cent?
- Which qualities should cost more than others? Why?
- What things might reduce the cost of a quality?
- What things might increase the cost of a quality?
- Are there any qualities that will ALWAYS cost the most/least?

Work with your child/ren to allocate the prices to the qualities for life. Make sure to challenge them to explore reasons, alternatives, and any exceptions to the rule. Consider influencing factors such as these:

- Is 'family' worth more or less if you get on well with them or not?
- Are 'friends' worth more or less depending on how many you have?
- Does the value and therefore the cost of 'education' change according to how good it is? If so, what makes it good or not so good?
- Is 'food and water' worth more if it is clean and fresh?

Taking all of this into account, do you need to add any additional information to your 'qualities' cards in order to justify the cost you have allocated to them?

Qualities for a good life

Health	Food and water	Entertainment	Family
Friends	Freedom	Peace	Love

Sleep	Happiness	Education	Money
Time	Self-confidence	Technology	Nature / The environment

Price tags

1 p/cent	5 p/cent	10 p/cent	50 p/cent
£1/$1	£5/$5	£10/$20	£20/$20
£50/$50	£100/$100	£200/$200	£500/$500
£1000/$1000	£10,000/$10,000	£100,000/$100,000	£1 million / $1 million

Cost chronicles

Challenge your child/ren to write three different cost-related stories, poems, or comics.

- One story should be about something very small and rather insignificant-looking but very expensive.
- Another should be about something very large, fancy, and impressive to look at but not worth very much at all.
- The third should be about something so precious and unique that you cannot buy it.

Cost currency

Over the course of the week or a few days encourage your child/ren to do jobs, complete tasks, use manners, follow rules, etc. in exchange for being paid. Their payment, however, comes in the form of buttons. Make sure that the buttons you use to 'pay' them with are varied in colour, size, material, etc.

By the end of the week your child/ren should have a fair size bundle of buttons. Encourage them to think about how these buttons could represent some form of currency that they could use to trade back with you for treats or rewards.

- Do all the buttons have the same value?
- Are larger buttons worth twice the value of smaller buttons?
- Are metal buttons or shiny ones worth more than plastic ones?
- Do buttons with more holes have more value?

Encourage them to devise a visual key to explain how their 'currency' works.

Together, work out the 'cost' of different treats or rewards that your child/ren can then use their buttons to buy for themselves.

Mystery – How should Alice spend her money?

A Mystery is a problem-solving activity based on a central question. Clues are shared that help the participant develop a reasonable answer. The clues provide information that may be helpful but may, at times, be conflicting. This encourages flexible thinking and puts children in a space where they have to defend and explain their thinking.

The clue cards are divided into two sets. You may choose to use only set #1 (white) if you are working with very young children. If you choose to use both sets, start with set #1 and only introduce set #2 (grey) after you have discussed the following questions with set #1 cards. This way you can talk about how and why their thinking changes after looking at the cards in set #2.

First, encourage your child to sort and categorise the cards in whatever way makes sense to them, then ask the following questions about organising the clues:

- Is all of the information relevant/useful? Is some information more/less useful than other information?

- How could you sort the information or organise it so that it is easier to deal with? (For example, create different sets of information – all about Alice, all about Mary, all about money, etc.)

- Is there any missing information that would help us to advise Alice? (For example, what expenses does Mary have? What is Mary saving up for? Is there a library close to where Alice lives? Can Alice get an electronic version of her book cheaper? Does Alice like the girls who have asked her to hang out with them? etc.)

Then encourage your child to use the clues to answer the following:

- How much money should Alice contribute to her grandmother's gift?

- Should Alice and Mary share the cost of their grandmother's gift equally?

- Should Mary pay more because she is older? If yes, then should she also receive more money because she is older?

Alice is 11 years old

Alice is worried about making new friends at school

Alice gets £10/$12 every week from her parents for doing jobs around the house

The next in the series of Alice's favourite books is out next week

It is Alice's grandmother's 60th birthday in 2 weeks

Alice and Mary stop off on the way home from school so Alice can buy the sweets she loves

Alice and Mary plan to buy a gift for their grandmother together

Alice promised Andy she would send him a gift every month

Alice has £15/$19 saved so far

The girls at school are all collecting friendship bracelets in different colours

Alice doesn't have a friendship bracelet

Reading always makes Alice feel good.

Alice's sister Mary is
15 years old

Alice just started her
new school 2 weeks
ago.

Mary has been saving
her money and has
£50/$62 saved up

The gift for Alice and
Mary's grandmother
costs £24/$30

Alice's favourite books
cost £5.99 each

Mary gets £10/$12
each week for helping
around the house

Alice has a best friend,
Andy, at her old school
and doesn't want him to
forget her

Alice has been invited
to go shopping with 2
girls from school

Trendy friendship
bracelets cost £7/$9
each

The girls at Alice's new school like to hang out at the shops and buy sweets

Mary gets extra money each week if she walks Alice home after school

Alice's favourite sweets cost £1/ $1.25

Alice's grandmother loves reading too and they spend lots of time together looking at books

Lessons to support learning

Fairy tale cost – 'Jack and the Beanstalk'

Share the story 'Jack and the Beanstalk' with your children. There are many versions out there aimed at all age ranges as well as animations and dramatisations of the story, and any will work.

YouTube version: www.youtube.com/watch?v=9q1dfTOoSrA

After sharing the story, work with your child/ren to identify all the references to cost within the story.

Examples may include the following:

- *The cost of the milk they sold from their cow was their only income.*

- *They needed to pay the cost to have their damaged house fixed.*

- *Jack's mother said that the cow should cost at least five gold coins for someone to buy her at market.*

- *Jack's mother insisted that she should not be sold for a smaller price/cost.*

- *The man on the road tells Jack that five magic beans are worth more than five gold coins.*

- *Jack is told that the beans will make him richer than he could imagine.*

- *Jack decided that the magic beans could pay for the cost of fixing the roof, the windows, and the front door AND buy a new cow.*

- *Jack sold the cow for the cost of five magic beans.*

- *The cost to Jack of not coming home with five gold coins was that his mother was very angry with him.*

- *His mother thought the beans were worth nothing and threw them out of the window.*

- *The cost to Jack's feelings was that he was now sad, feeling guilty and stupid.*

- *Jack's curiosity to climb the beanstalk costs him his safety.*

- *The giant's foolishness cost him his five gold coins, a hen that lays golden eggs, and a golden harp.*

- *The giant's huge size and slowness cost him the opportunity to catch Jack.*
- *Jack chopping down the beanstalk cost the Giant his ability to return to his castle and his wife.*
- *Jack's guilt about the giant's sadness cost him his own happiness.*

Questions to explore the theme of cost in the story:
- *What do you think the biggest example of cost is in this fairy tale?*
- *What are the similarities and differences between cost and loss in the story?*
- *What are the examples of personal cost in the story?*
- *Which character suffers the greatest personal cost?*
- *What are the examples of monetary cost (money) in the story?*
- *Which character suffers the most monetary cost?*
- *Are there any examples of natural or environmental cost in the story?*
- *What might be the impact of not carefully weighing up the costs and benefits of our actions?*
- *What can we learn from this story about cost?*
- *What costs do you have in your day-to-day life?*

Concept target

Together with your child/ren, create a list of vocabulary related to the concept of cost.

Here is a list of related vocabulary to start you off using the concept target. It would be great if you and your child could add to this list or make your own list. Remember to draw on your discussions from some of the other activities to help to evaluate each word or term.

- Cost
- Price
- Money
- Bargain
- Payment
- Spending
- Buy
- Saving

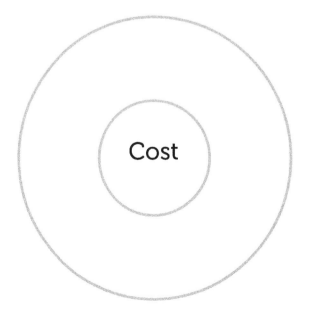

Venn diagram with cost

Have everyone in the family brainstorm three to five words or phrases they think of when they hear the term 'cost' and three to five words or phrases they think of when they hear the term 'value'. Then place the phrases on a Venn diagram:

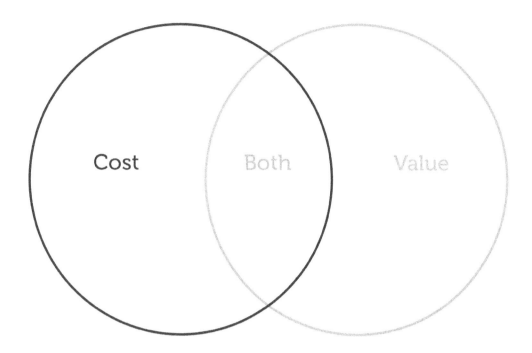

Saving cost? Baking cookies

Conduct an experiment to see if it saves money to bake your own cookies. When you are at the store, look at the cost of a pack of cookies and help your child figure out what it costs per dozen or per cookie. Then use the following recipe (or a family favourite) and do your best to figure out the total cost per dozen or per cookie.

Cookie recipe

- 1 1/2 cups / 210 g all-purpose flour
- 1/2 teaspoon baking soda / bicarbonate of soda
- 1/4 teaspoon salt
- 1/2 cup / 1 stick / 113 g unsalted butter, at room temperature
- 1/2 cup / 175 g maple syrup
- 1/2 cup / 85 g brown sugar
- 1 large egg
- 1/4 teaspoon vanilla bean paste
- 1 1/2 cups / 263 g dark or milk chocolate chips
- 1 teaspoon flaky sea salt

Directions

1   In a small bowl, whisk together flour, baking soda, and salt. Set aside.

2   Combine the butter, maple sugar, and brown sugar together in a standing mixer or with a hand-held mixer. Mix until creamy and airy.

3   Add egg and vanilla. Slowly pour in the flour mixture and mix until combined. Fold in the chocolate chips and chill in the refrigerator one hour to overnight.

4   Preheat the oven to 350°F/180°C. Line a baking sheet with parchment paper or silicone mats.

5   Using an ice cream scoop, drop batter onto baking sheet two inches apart.

6   Sprinkle with flaky sea salt and bake for ten minutes, or until golden brown. Cool on a wire rack or eat warm with a glass of milk.

Cost comparison

- What was most challenging about calculating the cost of baking cookies?

- Which cost more, buying cookies or making them?

- What are some of the other benefits besides cost of making your own cookies? Of buying cookies at the store?

- Are there certain occasions when one choice is better than the other?

Other costs

Think and talk about whether or not there are other costs to consider. For example:

- Is there an environmental cost to buying cookies – extra packaging, trucks used to deliver the cookies, etc.? Is there an environmental cost to baking cookies?
- Which one has more cost in terms of time? How is the time different?
- Are there health costs to consider? Allergens, extra preservatives, etc.?
- Would there be a cost of lost jobs if we ALWAYS baked cookies?

I wonder

Children are naturally curious. They have lots of questions, which helps them to understand their world. Help your child to not only maintain this natural tendency but also build on it. Throughout the week, make 'I wonder' statements and then work with your child to come up with at least ten questions that would help both of you to learn more. For example, you might say, 'I wonder why some sunsets are more colourful than others'.

Then you would ask your child what questions they could ask to learn more. Examples include the following:

- What causes the colours to appear during a sunset?
- Are sunsets affected by the weather?
- Do sunsets appear differently during different seasons?
- Is there something in the air that causes the colours of the sunset?
- Are colourful sunsets related to rainbows?

Five frame / Ten frame

If you have a preschooler, it is best to start with a five frame, but if you have an early primary student, you can start with a ten frame. Here are a couple of options for creating your five/ten frames:

- Cut the end off of an egg carton so that you have two rows of five to create a ten frame, and then cut that in half to create a five frame.
- Draw a five frame or ten frame with sidewalk chalk outside or on a piece of paper.

Gather five or ten small objects like buttons or coins. Work with your child to 'make 5 or 10', and then write it as an addition problem.

For example:

- Place three buttons in the five frame and count how many more buttons you would need to fill the frame. Write $3 + 2 = 5$.
- Place six buttons in the ten frame and count how many more buttons you would need to fill the frame. Write $6 + 4 = 10$.

Write as many facts as you can. Talk about the fact that $3 + 2$ and $2 + 3$ both equal 5, and see if your child can explain why.

Idea One:
Taking risks can have profound negative consequences

Idea Two:
Not taking risks has negative psychological consequences

Dinner table conversations

Concept: Risk

Main question: What is risk?

Follow-up questions:

- Is risk a good thing or a bad thing? Why?
- Is something that is risky always a risk?
- Should we always avoid risk?
- Does something have to be dangerous to be a risk?
- What are some risks you have taken? Would you change anything about what you did?
- When does risk help us?

Concept: Risk

Main question: Why do games involve risk?

Follow-up questions:

- How do games involve risk?
- What kinds of risk are we talking about?
- Can you think of a game that doesn't have any risk?

- Would you still enjoy playing a game if there were was no risk at all?
- As you learn a game does it have less risk? Does a game have less risk if you have played it a lot?
- Do you have to take risks to win games?

Concept: Risk

Main question: What is the difference between taking a risk and being reckless?

Follow-up questions:
- What does it mean to be reckless?
- What other words might we use for 'reckless'?
- Is taking a risk always reckless?
- What could we do to make sure taking a risk was not reckless?
- How do we know if we are taking a risk?
- What is the relationship between risk and danger?
- What is the relationship between risk and safety?
- Why might people take risks?

Concept: Risk

Main question: What are the main risks we face today?

Follow-up questions:

- Are these the same risks we faced yesterday / last week / last month / last year?
- Will the risks be the same tomorrow / next week / next month?
- Are these risks the same for everybody?
- Who is responsible for managing these risks?
- How do you manage these risks?
- How do we know which are the biggest risks and which are the smallest?
- Do we deal with big and small risks in the same way?
- How might the risks you face change as you get older?

Trust walk

Talk about the relationship between risk and trust. For example, if you trust the people around you, do you believe you are less at risk?

Do a trust walk in the house or outside. Blindfold a family member and direct them to find different items using only verbal instructions.

Risk assessment scavenger hunt

Have your child/ren go around the house and look for things or places in the house that have risks. Challenge them to find a certain number of risks. They can write them down, draw pictures of them, or take pictures of them.

Later that day or the next day, talk about the risks. Ask questions like these: 'What made you decide it was a risk?' 'Is it always a risk?' 'How can we minimise the risk?'

Come up with a plan to address the risks.

Group game – SKUNK

This would be a great game to play on video chats with friends or family members. Here is what you do:

- Everyone writes SKUNK across the top of a page and draws vertical lines between each letter to make columns.

- One person rolls two dice and calls out the numbers.

- Everyone adds them (or multiplies them, if you want to adapt for older children) and writes the sum (or multiple) under the S.

- After every roll, each person must decide to 'stay in' or 'settle'. If they stay in, they are in for another roll, but if they settle, then their score for the letter S is the sum of whatever they have in that column/letter.

- If a double is rolled, anyone who is still 'in' is skunked and has to cross off all numbers for that column/letter.

- You are done with a letter whenever a double is rolled or everyone settles. If a double is rolled on the first roll, everyone is skunked for that letter and no one receives points for it.

Repeat the same process for each letter. At the end, whoever has the highest total score (adding the sums for each letter) wins the game.

Art activity

Have your child/ren create a poster detailing the risks of not washing your hands properly.

They could draw around their hand in the centre of the page and write a key risk factor on each finger. Between the fingers and around the hand could be tips and pointers (see what we did there ☺) of what can be done to minimise these risks as much as possible. They could use the internet to search for related data and facts. You can then hang the picture up in your bathroom or kitchen where people wash their hands a lot.

Fairy tale risks – 'Little Red Riding Hood'

Share the story 'Little Red Riding Hood' with your children. There are many versions out there aimed at all age ranges as well as animations and dramatisations of the story, and any will work.

The following are two YouTube versions that you may use:

Animated version on YouTube: www.youtube.com/watch?v=LDMWJCrDVMl&t=22s

Book-based version on YouTube: www.youtube.com/watch?v=MOHAUkgh4Es

After sharing the story, work with your child/ren to identify all the risks within the story.

Examples may include the following:

- *Red Riding Hood walked through the woods even though she knew there was wolf in the woods.*
- *Red Riding Hood didn't stick to the path but ventured off to pick flowers.*
- *Red Riding Hood talked to the 'stranger' she met in the woods.*
- *Red Riding Hood told the 'stranger' her plans.*
- *Grandma invited the wolf into her cottage before checking to see who it was first.*
- *Red Riding Hood entered the cottage even though she was suspicious that it didn't sound like Grandma inviting her in.*
- *Red Riding Hood continued to stay in the cottage despite her suspicions that all didn't look right.*

Questions to explore the theme of risk in the story:

- *Should Red Riding Hood have taken the risk to visit Grandma? Why? Why not?*
- *Which was the biggest risk she took?*
- *How could she have still taken the same risks but stayed safe?*
- *How might some risks have been more careless than others?*
- *What risks did the wolf take?*
- *What risks did the woodcutter take?*
- *Why did some risks pay off and others didn't?*
- *How do we know if a risk is worth taking or not?*
- *What might be the impact of never taking any risks? Is this even possible?*
- *What can we learn from this story about risk-taking?*
- *How might this relate to our lives today?*

Concept target

Together with your child/ren, create a list of vocabulary related to the concept of risk.

Here is a list of related vocabulary to start you off using the concept target. It would be great if you and your child could add to this list or make your own list. Remember to draw on your discussions from some of the other activities to help to evaluate each word or term.

- Danger
- Threat
- Opportunity
- Chance
- Adventure
- Problem
- Challenge

Risk

Free time probability

Ask your child to name three things that he or she would like to do for fun each day during shared free time with you. Then you think of two jobs/chores that you would like your child to help you complete during shared free time. Cut five strips of paper and write one activity or job/chore on each strip. Put all of them in a cup and plan to draw one strip out each day.

Before drawing a strip each day, ask your child what the chance/probability/risk is that they will being doing one of their chosen activities versus a job/chore that you have chosen. Then talk about different ways to express that chance/probability. For example, on the first day, they have a three out of five chance. That could also be expressed as a 60% chance of doing one of their activities or a 40% risk of doing a job/chore. On the second day, they will have a three out of four chance or a two out of four chance, depending on what was chosen on the first day.

Ask questions like the following:

- Is there a difference between risk and chance?
- Is there any risk involved for me when you draw a slip?
- Is there any risk of drawing a slip that we won't be able to do today?
- How is it easier to predict what might be chosen as the week goes on?
- On what day does any risk or chance disappear from the activity?
- What is more interesting, risk or certainty? Why?

Risk assessment

Complete a risk assessment using the question prompts to assess the overall risk factor of each action. Encourage your child to consider not only the obvious risks but also any unusual and unexpected risks that might be connected to variations of the same action.

What are the probable risks? (Think about the obvious, everyday risks that first come to mind.)

What are the possible risks? (Think about things that COULD happen that you didn't first think of, especially if the situations change.)

What are some of the unlikely risks? (Think creatively about risks that might be very unlikely, but could still happen in certain circumstances.)

For example, for riding a bike:

Probable risks might include falling off or not being able to stop.

Possible risks might include riding in traffic and crossing in front of a car, riding on bumpy ground and hitting a rock, or your chain falling off of the gears.

Unlikely risks might include riding an adult bike when you can barely touch the pedals, riding on ice and slipping, or a wheel coming loose and falling off.

Once you have answered the questions, talk about how much risk there is based on the probability of the listed risks. Assign a score between 1% and 100%.

Washing your hands

What are the probable risks?
What are the possible risks?
What are the unlikely risks?

Risk score (0-100%)

©2020 www.challenginglearning.com

Crossing the road

What are the probable risks?
What are the possible risks?
What are the unlikely risks?

Risk score (0-100%)

©2020 www.challenginglearning.com

Eating fruit

What are the probable risks?
What are the possible risks?
What are the unlikely risks?

Risk score (0-100%)

©2020 www.challenginglearning.com

Owning a pet

What are the probable risks?
What are the possible risks?
What are the unlikely risks?

Risk score (0-100%)

©2020 www.challenginglearning.com

Going to school

What are the probable risks?
What are the possible risks?
What are the unlikely risks?

Risk score (0-100%)

©2020 www.challenginglearning.com

Reading a book

What are the probable risks?
What are the possible risks?
What are the unlikely risks?

Risk score (0-100%)

©2020 www.challenginglearning.com

Swimming

What are the probable risks?
What are the possible risks?
What are the unlikely risks?

Risk score (0-100%)

Playing with a friend

What are the probable risks?
What are the possible risks?
What are the unlikely risks?

Risk score (0-100%)

Talking to a stranger

What are the probable risks?
What are the possible risks?
What are the unlikely risks?

Risk score (0-100%)

Climbing a tree

What are the probable risks?
What are the possible risks?
What are the unlikely risks?

Risk score (0-100%)

Cutting with a knife

What are the probable risks?
What are the possible risks?
What are the unlikely risks?

Risk score (0-100%)

Playing with balloons

What are the probable risks?
What are the possible risks?
What are the unlikely risks?

Risk score (0-100%)

Write each statement on the following scale based on the risk score you have assigned:

100%

25%

50%

75%

0%

Questions to help encourage deeper dialogue

- Can anything be 100% risk? Can anything have 0% risk?

- What is considered a risk?

- Does risk always mean danger?

- What other kinds of risks can be associated with these actions?

- Are there safe risks? What might be considered a safe risk?

- If something is a 50% risk / 50% not risk, how is that different than 0% risk? Do they cancel each other out?

- How do you decide if one risk is a higher percentage than another?

- Can you think of any positive risks?

- Do you need to decide what your criteria is for risk before you can assess the overall risk score?

- How might the risk be different for different people?

- What part does age and experience play in calculating a risk score?

Other activities

- -

Counting money

Put out three bowls or plates and label them with a target amount of money. Place a combination of coins and notes/bills on the table and encourage your child to come up with at least three different combinations for each target. For each combination, have them count out the money to double check.

Ask questions like the following:

- Which combinations are easier to count? Why?

- Why do you think we have coins and notes/bills with different values? Why do you think we have the values that we do?

- Are there some coins or notes/bills that are more useful? Which ones?

- If you could only have one type of coin or note/bill, what would you choose? Why?

Story writing

- -

Take five random photographs or draw five things from around the house or outside and use them to create a story. For younger children, have them tell you the story, and for older children, have them do the writing. If you have children of multiple ages, they can work together to create and write the story.

To guide their thinking, before they write the story, ask questions like these:

- Where and when will your story take place?

- Will there be characters in your story? Will they be real or made-up?

- Will there be a problem or challenge in your story? How will it be resolved?

- How might you end your story?

LESSON 7 BIG QUESTION – WHAT IS TIME?

Idea One:
You can't stop the clock or change time

Idea Two:
You can make time for things

Time

Dinner table conversations

Concept: Time

Main question: What is time?

Follow-up questions:

- How do we know that time exists? What makes time real?
- Are the past and the future real?
- How would you describe time to someone who doesn't know what it is?
- Can you see time? Can you draw it?
- How important is it to know the time?
- Who decides how we use our time?
- Does time have a beginning and an end? When? Where?

Concept: Time

Main question: What is free time?

Follow-up questions:

- Can time really be free? When is it free?
- Who puts a value on time?
- What is the cost of time?
- What control do we have over how we spend our time?

- Is it possible to do absolutely nothing for any length of time?
- How would you describe free time?
- How important is free time?
- Can you always *make* time for something important?
- Is it ever possible to have no time?
- Is it possible to have too much time?

Concept: Time

Main question: How do we use time?

Follow-up questions:

- When are you 'on time'?
- Can you be 'off time'?
- What does it mean to be early or late?
- Who decides if time is wasted?
- What is a 'good' use of time?
- Who controls your use of time?
- Can you control other people's use of time?
- What role does your memory have in your use of time?
- What role do your dreams have in your use of time? Where do they fit – past, present, or future?

Concept: Time

Main question: Would it be good to be able to control the movement of time?

Follow-up questions:

- If you could stop and restart time, what would you do and why?
- How far into the future/past would you like to travel?
- Which famous person from the past would you most like to meet? Why?
- If you could only ask them five questions, what would they be?
- What problems might there be if we were all able to control the movement of time?
- Does time ever move the same for us all? What about insects, animals, babies, old people?

Picture book activity

Tuesday by David Wiesner is a good book to discuss the concept of time. It can be found in a bookstore, the library, or online.

Download lesson ideas from the Challenging Learning Website here:

www.challenginglearning.com/product/picture-books-tuesday/.

Chalk circle clock

Use chalk to draw a large circle outside. Have your child/ren draw the numbers 1–12 where they would go on a clock, then in another colour, add marks for the minutes.

Either find sticks of different sizes to use as the hour hand and minute hand, or have an older child represent the minute hand and a younger child represent the hour hand.

Alternate between setting up a time and asking your children to tell you what the time is and giving them a time and asking them to arrange the sticks or people to show that time.

Talk about what you might be doing at the different times over the course of a day.

Group game – What's the time, Wise Old Wolf?

This is a game to play with the whole family. Here is how you play:

- Choose one person to be Wise Old Wolf. That person stands at one end of the playing area with his/her back to everyone else.

- The other players line up, facing Wise Old Wolf, at the other end of the playing area.

- The players call out 'What's the time, Wise Old Wolf?' and Wise Old Wolf answers with a time (e.g., five o'clock), then the other players take that many steps towards Wise Old Wolf.

This is repeated until Wise Old Wolf responds with 'It's dinner time!' and then chases the other players back to the starting line. If Wise Old Wolf tags anyone, they become Wise Old Wolf, and the game starts over.

Time travel

OPTIONAL: View the story of Urashima, a Japanese legend about a time-travelling fisherman. View on YouTube: www.youtube.com/watch?v=SSBTBX5juLE.

Talk about time travel and ask your child if they would like to be able to travel through time. Use questions like the following:

- What time period would you like to go to? Why?

- Would there be risks to time travel?

- What might happen if you go to the past and change something that impacts current time?

- Is there a problem with knowing what will happen in the future? What if you change what you do based on what you learned?

Collect recycled materials or items you have thrown away and design a time machine. Make up a story about what you will do with the time machine. Think about where you will go, what will happen, if you will be able to come back, if things will change, etc.

Fairy tale time – 'Cinderella'

Share the story 'Cinderella' with your children. There are many versions out there aimed at all age ranges as well as animations and dramatisations of the story, and any will work. The following are two YouTube versions that you may use:

Animated: www.youtube.com/watch?v=BXDsucz23OA

Book-based: www.youtube.com/watch?v=0Z6ha1UWt3w

After sharing the story, work with your child/ren to talk about how time is used in the story.

Example topics may include the following:

- *Cinderella spent most of her time cleaning and taking care of her stepmother and stepsisters. How do you think she would have liked to spend her time? How would you feel if that is how you spent most of your time? Is this a good use of time?*

- *Cinderella did not have much time to prepare for the ball. What challenges did this create? How might the story have been different if she had a lot of time?*

- *Cinderella had to leave the ball by a certain time. How would the story have been different if she could have stayed as long as she wanted at the ball?*

- *Could you write an alternative ending to the story where Cinderella had as long as she wanted at the ball?*

Additional 'Cinderella' activity: Summing up in a caption

Challenge everyone in the family to write a version of 'Cinderella' in 50 words. It can be a modern take, a twist on the story, a poem, or an amusing ditty.

For example: Cinderella gazed amazed as her fairy godmother turned the pumpkin into a silver and sparkly carriage. Two white mice became handsome horses. She slid into her slippers, started to climb the steps and exclaimed, 'I've changed my mind, so sorry! I just want to stay home and finish my book'.

Comparing time

Compare the amount of time it takes to do a particular task in different ways, for example, peeling a banana with one hand, with two hands, with your mouth, blindfolded, with a knife and fork, etc. Which was quickest? How much quicker? Why? Is there a quicker way? Is it always best to do it the quickest way?

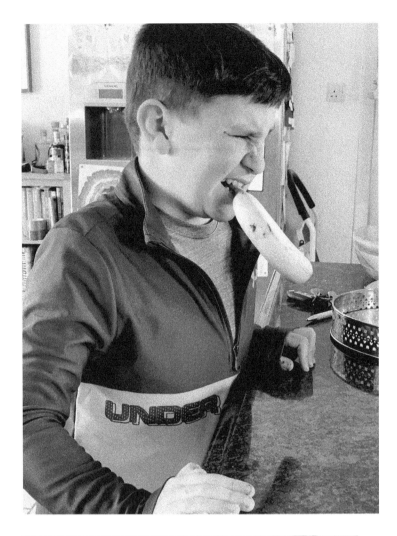

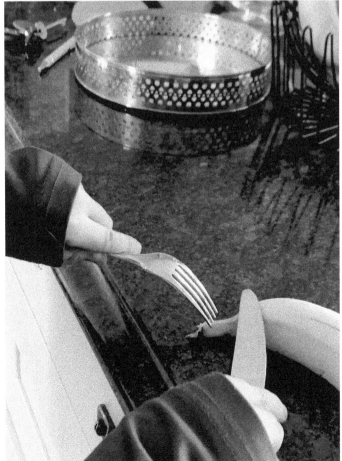

Lessons to support learning

Concept target

Together with your child/ren, create a list of vocabulary related to the concept of time.

Here is a list of related vocabulary to start you off using the concept target. It would be great if you and your child could add to this list or make your own list. Remember to draw on your discussions from some of the other activities to help to evaluate each word or term.

- Hours
- Minutes
- Clock
- Routine
- Priorities
- Planning
- Organisation
- Schedule

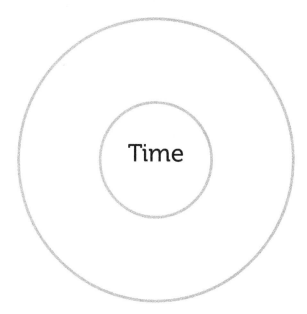

Growing over time

Talk with your child about growing plants, flowers, or vegetables from seeds. Talk about the time it takes for the seed to grow under the soil, to sprout through the soil, to become a plant large enough to have leaves and flowers, to produce fruit or vegetables, etc. Plant something together and have your child create a growing journal to document the experience.

Needed: compost / planting soil, plastic tub or pot, seeds (the pictures show children growing potatoes), spade/trowel, watering can, paper for growing journal, markers/pens

Suggested directions

- After gathering the materials, create a booklet by folding three or four pieces of paper in half (you can staple the centre or you can poke holes and run string through the holes) and decorate the cover.

- Make predictions about how long it will take for the plant to sprout through the soil, to grow more than 2 cm, to flower, etc.

- Use the booklet to describe what you do and what you learn and to make daily observations.

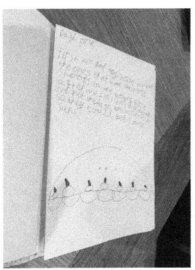

Time graph

For one day, keep a diary of everything your child does during the day. Indicate the start and stop time of everything they do – getting dressed, eating breakfast, reading stories, playing, eating lunch, etc. For example:

> 6:00 a.m. – 6:15 a.m. – got dressed
>
> 6:30 a.m. – 7:15 a.m. – ate breakfast
>
> 7:15 a.m. – 7:45 a.m. – read stories
>
> 7:45 a.m. – 8:30 a.m. – played with blocks
>
> Etc.

The next day, decide on categories for the activities your child engaged in the day before. For example, you can have self-care, eating, playing, reading, sleeping, watching TV, and school work. You and your child can decide which categories fit best. Once you have decided on the categories, figure out how many minutes your child spent in each category.

Use the following time graph and write the categories you have selected along the bottom, then colour in a box for every five minutes that was spent in that category. Talk about the following:

- Is there anything that surprised you? Why?

- Did you spend the most amount of time doing things you like to do?

- Is there something you would like to spend more time doing? How can we make that happen?

- Are there some things that you think you spent too much time doing? How can we change that for tomorrow?

- What was your best use of time?

Time Graph

Minutes spent on the activity

150 min
145 min
140 min
135 min
130 min
125 min
120 min
115 min
110 min
105 min
100 min
95 min
90 min
85 min
80 min
75 min
70 min
65 min
60 min
55 min
50 min
45 min
40 min
35 min
30 min
25 min
20 min
15 min
10 min
5 min

Moving it

Get your child/ren moving by timing them doing different activities.

See how long they can do the following:

- Hop on one foot
- Balance on one leg
- Hold a plank
- Hula hoop

Or see how many of these exercises they can do in one minute:

- Sit-ups
- Push-ups
- Jumping jacks
- Star jumps

Challenge them to make predictions, keep improving, beat their best time, etc.

Minute to Win It

For a fun family game, come up with various Minute to Win It tasks. These are tasks that you will all do at once for one minute to see who can do the most/best.

Here are some examples:

- Stack coins – Who can stack the most?
- Stack cups – Who can make the highest free-standing tower?
- Pick up cereal pieces using a straw and place them in a cup – Who can pick up the most?
- Flying feather – Who can keep a feather in the air for whole minute simply by blowing it? It must not touch any body part or the ground.

Mystery – Does Holly have time to join the swim club?

Holly is interested in joining the swim team at the local swim club. She is trying to decide if she has enough time to take on this new commitment. Use the information on the following cards to help her make this decision.

Holly's family lives 30 minutes from the swimming pool.

Holly's brother, Jack plays hockey and football in Bloomington.

Holly is 10 years old.

At school, Holly has swim class every Friday.

Holly was only on the hockey club for a month.

Julie only has two Magic Mermaid dolls to buy in order to have the whole set.

In Holly's house, when you turn 10, you must help at Posh Paws.

Holly's mom runs a dog grooming business, called Posh Paws

Jack is 13 years old.

Holly's sister, sister Sarah is 18 years old and has her own car.

Each week, Holly has jobs to do for her parents around the house.

Holly's history homework usually takes at least an hour.

Holly's Dad has
an office in
Bloomington.

Magic Mermaids is on
TV six days a week.

Posh Paws is based at
Holly's house.

Holly's family has dinner
with her grandparents
each Sunday.

Holly has a favourite
TV show called Magic
Mermaids.

Holly is saving up to
purchase the new
Magic Mermaid dolls.

The swim club has
practices available every
evening.

Holly and her grandma
have been learning
to paint as a shared
activity on Sundays.

To be class monitor,
you have to be
prepared to give up
time to help in the
classroom.

Holly desperately wants to be as good of a swimmer as the Mermaids on her show.

To be on the swim club, the swimmers need to go to 3 practices a week.

Any practices scheduled on the weekend are at pools in other towns.

Holly's teacher made her the class monitor for this term.

Julie hates swimming and is afraid of water.

Holly's best friend is called Julie.

When she was 6 years old, Holly joined the hockey club.

In the next month or so, Julie's parents are moving next door to Holly

There are 5 dolls in the Magic Mermaid doll set.

Holly enjoys her time at her grandparent's house.

Holly gets £3 per hour for helping at Posh Paws.

Two of Holly's neighbours swim at the swim club.

Magic Mermaid dolls cost £25.

Julie and Holly love hanging out whenever they can.

The main swimming pool is in Bloomington town centre.

Each swim practice is an hour and a half long.

Holly gets homework every night from school.

Holly's dad coaches Jack's hockey team.

Sarah has a new
boyfriend called
Michael.

Holly's most confident
stroke is the
breaststroke.

Holly has not yet
learned to ride a bike.

Use the following questions to deepen the dialogue:

- How did you sort the cards to organise the information?
- What are some of the factors that would influence Holly's decision?
- What connections did you make between the different pieces of information?
- What information do you feel is missing? What questions do you still have?
- Was there any irrelevant information?
- What inferences did you make from the information shared?
- What do you think was the most important piece of information? How does this influence your thinking?
- What would your response be to Holly?

LESSON 8 BIG QUESTION – WHAT IS THEFT/STEALING?

Idea One:
Only bad people steal

Idea Two:
Most people in their lifetime will have stolen something

Dinner table conversations

Concept: Stealing

Main question: What is stealing?

Follow-up questions:

- Is it still stealing if we take items that don't belong to anyone?
- What is the difference between stealing something and taking something?
- Is stealing only stealing if someone intends to do it?
- Is stealing always a deliberate act?
- What is the difference between stealing and cheating?
- What is the difference between stealing and borrowing?
- Are there things beyond objects that can be stolen?
- Stealing a base, stealing the show, stealing a kiss, stealing an item. What do all these forms of stealing have in common?

Concept: Stealing

Main question: Is stealing always wrong?

Follow-up questions:

- Can you name any positive types of stealing?
- If you take five minutes longer for your lunch break, is that stealing? Is it always wrong?

- If you say 'sorry', does that make stealing acceptable?
- What type of stealing is the worst of all?
- What would be the worst thing to have stolen from you?
- Why might we forgive some people who steal and not others?
- Should stealing always be forgiven?
- Should stealing always be punished?
- Did Robin Hood do the right thing by stealing from the rich and giving to the poor?
- If you find some money and keep it, is that better or worse than finding it and giving it to charity?
- Is stealing something valuable worse than stealing something of no value?

Concept: Stealing

Main question: Why do people steal?

Follow-up questions:

- What are the different reasons for stealing?
- Who decides what a 'thief' is?
- Is it possible to steal and not be a thief?
- When is stealing a necessary act?
- Do some people have more of a right to steal than others?
- Fake designer labels and counterfeit goods – do these represent stealing? If so, who is doing the stealing and from whom?
- Does stealing make you a bad person?
- Should we always forgive children who steal?
- Should stealing be judged morally or criminally?
- Is it okay to steal if your needs are more important than others'?

Concept: Stealing

Main question: Is it possible to have a world with no stealing?

Follow-up questions:

- If money didn't exist, would that end stealing?
- Is it possible to steal from someone who has no possessions?
- Would a world without stealing be a better place to live?
- Is it possible for someone to go through their whole life without stealing?
- How would the world be different if it was acceptable to steal?
- When might stealing make the world more fair?
- Is stealing still wrong if it helps other people?
- If thieves only stole from strangers rather than people they knew, would this make it okay?
- If your human rights have been stolen, should you aim to steal them back?

Picture book activity

The Teddy Robber by Ian Beck is a book about a little boy trying to solve the mystery of who snatched his teddy in the middle of the night.

YouTube version: www.youtube.com/watch?v=-7HoXkY_r78.

Use the following questions to discuss the book with your child.

- What would you say to the giant if you were Tom?
- If someone returns what they have stolen, does that make it okay?

- Is there a reason for every action?

- Would it be possible to steal anything if we didn't have possessions?

- Is stealing ever right?

- Is it okay to take back something that has been stolen, or is it still stealing?

Exploring theft/stealing

Use the cards to engage in the following explorations:

Opinion line – Here you can use an opinion line with the cards to help your child build their own understanding about stealing. Start out by asking your child what they think stealing is. Jot down their ideas and come up with a definition of stealing. Arrange the cards on an opinion line from 'strongly agree' to 'strongly disagree' that the act on the card is an example of stealing.

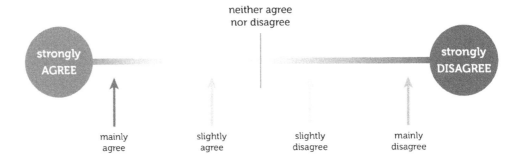

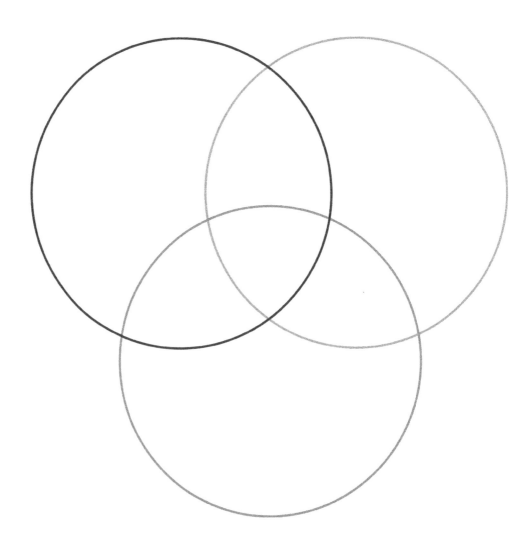

Venn diagram – Create a three-concept Venn diagram like the one pictured, where the blue is **borrowing**, the red is **stealing**, and the green is *sharing*. Where two colours overlap, place cards that can be examples of both terms, and in the centre where all three circles overlap, place cards that can be described by all three terms.

Ranking – Rank the cards in order from the most serious to the least serious. Allow for multiple cards to be ranked at the same level if needed.

When completing each exploration, ask questions like the following: 'Why did you place that card there?' 'Would that always be true?' 'Have you ever experienced anything like that? How did it make you feel?' 'Why do you think someone would do that?' 'Does it matter who does it?'

Picking a flower that is growing in the park	Taking a school pen or pencil home	Taking a TV that someone has put out as rubbish/garbage	Taking an apple from the supermarket without paying for it	Picking berries from a bush at the side of the pavement or road
Finding money on the ground and keeping it	Taking someone's wallet from their pocket	Giving someone an unexpected kiss without their permission	Pretending someone else's ideas are your own	Buying something from someone at a very cheap price
Taking possession of the ball from the opposing team in sport (e.g., basketball)	Drawing attention away from everyone else at an event	Glancing at someone and then looking away	Taking more paper napkins or straws than you need in a restaurant or café	Taking a shell from the beach
Breaking into someone's house and taking all of their valuables	Pretending you are somebody you are not (e.g., on social media)	Robbing a bank	Parking in someone else's parking spot	Secretly using your sister's perfume
Buying a pair of fake designer shoes	Taking something with permission but forgetting to give it back	Trading something with a friend but getting the better end of the deal	Using words from a different language or culture to your own	Eating a friend's sweets then giving them some of yours the following day
Wearing your friend's sunglasses because you forgot yours	Using your brother's colouring pencils	Taking eggs from chickens	Taking the neighbour's dog for a walk	Checking out a book from the library and taking it home

STEM exploration – stealing colour

Watch each glass of water steal colour from its neighbour to create new colours.

You will need the following:

Water

Six clear glasses or clear plastic beakers

Red, yellow, and blue food colouring

Six paper towels

- Fill three glasses about ¾ of the way up with water.
- Add a few drops of food colouring to each glass to make one cup of red water, one of blue, and one of green.
- Arrange the cups in a circle and put one empty cup between each coloured one.
- Fold each paper towel in half vertically and then in half again to make long strips.
- Place one end of the paper strip in an empty glass and the other in a glass filled with water.

- Place another in the same coloured water glass with the other end in the next empty glass.

- Keep going until all the glasses are linked together in this way by the paper towel strips.

- Notice how the paper towels start to absorb the water.

- Leave them overnight and witness how the water has moved or been stolen from the full glasses to the empty glasses and how it has mixed to form new colours.

The black and white thief – writing activity

'One for Sorrow' is a children's rhyme that comes from 16th-century Britain. It is a superstition rhyme that determines your fortune according to the number of magpies you see.

Magpies are famous as thieves in the bird world who not only steal eggs from other birds' nests but also steal bright, shiny objects and jewellery if they get the opportunity.

A 19th-century game keeper called Tom Speedy described this black and white bird in the following way:

'The magpie is one of the most expert, genteel and well-dressed thieves'.

Find out what you can about magpies. You could produce an informational poster on the bird or write a story in which a magpie steals something very valuable. Search online or in nursery rhyme books for the poem and read it with your child. Can you finish it off and write lines for seeing eight, nine, and ten magpies?

Rules of stealing

As a result of all of the activities and discussions, your children will begin to develop their own ideas about what stealing is. Here is an example of a conversation between a mum and a daughter walking on the beach:

> **Mum** – Is it considered stealing if we take shells from the beach?
>
> **Daughter** – No, because there are lots of them.
>
> **Mum** – If there is a lot of something, it is okay to take it? There are a lot of books at the bookstore. So, is it okay if I take some of them?
>
> **Daughter** – Well no, because they belong to the bookstore.
>
> **Mum** – Well who do the shells belong to?
>
> **Daughter** – They belong to the sea, and the sea doesn't mind if we take them.
>
> **Mum** – So, if you pick a flower at the park, would that be okay because it belongs to nature and nature won't mind?
>
> **Daughter** – Well, it depends on how many flowers there are. If there are a lot, it is okay, but if there is only one then it is not.
>
> **Mum** – Okay, if there are a lot of flowers, it is okay to take one?
>
> **Daughter** – Yes, well, it also depends on how big it is. It is okay to take a small one, but not a big one.

In this example, the daughter is making up her own rules about stealing within the context of the beach and shells. Engaging in a conversation like this helps children to develop their own thinking about rules and what is appropriate or acceptable. Choose a location – the beach, a park, your home, your child's room, etc. – and have a conversation with your child about what 'rules' there would be about stealing and encourage them to come up with their own set of rules. For example:

- In our home, it is not stealing if you take or use something that belongs to the whole family as long as everyone knows where it is and can still use it.

- In our home, it is not stealing food if you have asked mum and dad and they have said you can eat it.
- Borrowing my sister's clothes is not stealing as long as I don't damage them and I return them.

Once your child comes up with the rules, try to come up with counterexamples or questions to push their thinking. For the aforementioned rules, you can ask questions like these:

- How do we know what belongs to the whole family?
- Once you have asked permission to eat the food, is it okay to have as much as you want?
- Do you think you should ask permission to borrow your sister's clothes?
- Would you feel the same way about your brother borrowing your art supplies?

Concept square

Complete the chart with your own ideas and thoughts.

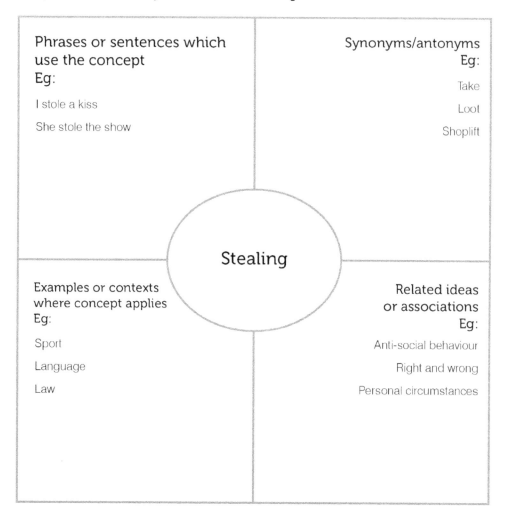

Phrases or sentences which use the concept Eg:	Synonyms/antonyms Eg:
I stole a kiss She stole the show	Take Loot Shoplift

Stealing

Examples or contexts where concept applies Eg:	Related ideas or associations Eg:
Sport Language Law	Anti-social behaviour Right and wrong Personal circumstances

The people vs Goldilocks!

Mystery – Is Goldilocks guilty or innocent of stealing (theft)?

Can you solve this Mystery and answer the question *Is Goldilocks guilty of stealing (theft)?* Explore the cards that follow to build an answer to this long-debated question. You may want to sort the information into sets to help you analyse and process it.

Goldilocks liked the look of the three bears' porridge so helped herself to it.

©2020 www.challenginglearning.com

Mummy bear was very unhappy that a stranger had ruined her clean bed linen

©2020 www.challenginglearning.com

The bears trusted everyone to behave well

©2020 www.challenginglearning.com

The bears had left their porridge to cool while they had a walk

©2020 www.challenginglearning.com

The 3 bears left their front door unlocked

©2020 www.challenginglearning.com

Goldilocks enters the bears' house without their consent

©2020 www.challenginglearning.com

Baby bear was very upset to have no porridge left at all

©2020 www.challenginglearning.com

Goldilocks was tired after chasing butterflies through the wood

©2020 www.challenginglearning.com

Goldilocks is below the age of 16

©2020 www.challenginglearning.com

Challenging LEARNING · Lessons to support learning

Goldilocks did not mean to break the chair

Goldilocks sits on a chair that is not hers and damages it.

Goldilocks had been sent off to do a job for her mother

The cost of new bed linen for 3 beds will be £200/$200

The value of the 3 bears' porridge would be less than £20/$20

Goldilocks checked to see if nobody was in the house before she went in

Goldilocks felt that any damage caused was all by accident

Goldilocks uses other people's property without their permission (beds)

Goldilocks knew that the house and all the things in it belonged to someone else

Goldilocks was hungry and had nowhere to go

On the three bears' return, Goldilocks ran off without saying she was sorry.

The three bears were looking forward to eating their porridge after their walk

She ruined 2 bowls of porridge and completely ate one of them

She sat on baby bears' chair knowing it was small and stayed sat until the bottom fell out of it.

Goldilocks snooped inside the three bears' private bedrooms

Questions

- Did Goldilocks commit a crime?
- Does the age of Goldilocks make a difference as to whether we see her as a thief or not?
- If Goldilocks were an adult, would you judge her actions differently?
- If Goldilocks were a male, would you judge his actions differently?
- How would you feel if a stranger came into your house and used and damaged your property?
- Did the bears do anything wrong?
- Were Goldilocks's actions motivated by greed or laziness or something else?
- If you use someone's property to the extent that they can't use it again, is this stealing?
- Is it still stealing if you do not remove it from the house?
- If you take something of someone else's and cannot return it in good condition, is this stealing?

Stealing in maths?

When completing some mathematical algorithms, the term 'take from the 10s place' or 'take from the 100s place' are sometimes used. For example, in the following subtraction problem, one option would be to solve it using a standard algorithm described in the following way:

You cannot subtract 5 from 4, so you 'take away' 1 ten and add it to the 1s place, then subtract 14–5, which is equal to 9. You cannot subtract 3 tens from the 1 ten that you have left, so you 'take away' one of the hundreds and add it to the 10s place, then subtract 11–3, which is equal to 8. Then you subtract the 1 hundred from the 1 hundred you have left. The answer to the problem is 89.

224
−135

Complete the following activity using the grids to help your child decide on different language for solving a standard algorithm. Or if they already use different language, like 'borrow' or 'trade', use the activity to help them to describe what they are doing.

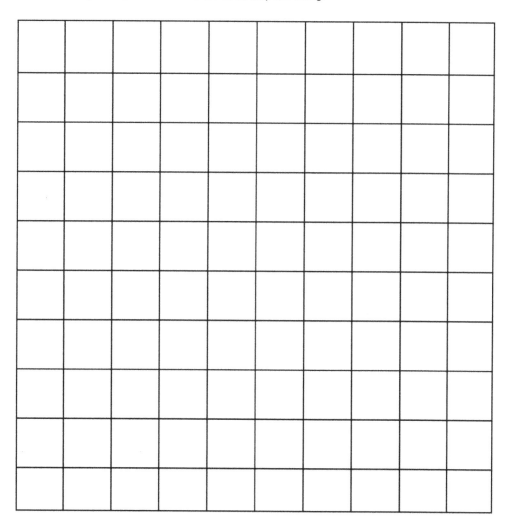

Colour the grids three different colours – the first one yellow, the second one a light blue, and the third one a light green. For younger children, you may want to create larger 10 x 10 grids.

Cut the light blue grid into ten strips of ten small squares, then cut the light green grid into 100 small squares. Talk to your child about what each of the colours represent. The yellow piece is 100 squares and represents the 100s place, the blue pieces are ten squares and represents the 10s place, and the green pieces are one square and represent the 1s place. Talk about how many green pieces fit on top of one blue piece, how many blue pieces fit on top of the yellow piece, etc.

Now work through the following tasks:

- Lay out seven green squares. Ask your child how many squares there are and have them write the number 7.

- Lay out two blue strips and three green squares. Ask your child how many total squares there are. Help them count as needed. Write the number 23 and talk about the fact that there are two blue strips and how the 2 is in the 10s place and there are three green squares and the 3 is in the 1s place.

  - Now lay out one of the blue strips and ask your child to lay out enough green squares to match the blue strip. Once they have placed ten green squares next to the blue strip, take the blue strip away so that you have one blue strip and 13 green squares.

  - Now ask your child how many squares there are. Help them count them if needed. Write the number 23 and ask your child to describe what happened. Ask them how they have the same number after you took away the green strip. Guide them to use phrases like 'I traded one 10 for ten 1s' or 'I made an exchange'. Emphasise the fact that the exchange was equal and did not change the value of the number, therefore nothing was 'taken away' or 'stolen'.

- Lay out the yellow piece and ask your child to come up with multiple ways to cover it up. For example, they could use three blue strips and 70 green squares, or six green strips and 40 green squares. Ask them if the value of three blue strips and 70 green squares is the same or different than the value of the yellow piece. Ask questions like the following:

  - What have you learned?

  - Why would we need to know about this?

  - How is this like money? How is it different from money?

  - Are there equal exchanges we can make with money?

Once you believe your child has a good understanding of the exchanges you can make within the 1s, 10s, and 100s places, solve subtraction problems like the one shown earlier and talk about what is happening at each step. Encourage your child to come up with a good way to describe what is happening by using words like 'trading' or 'exchanging' instead of 'taking away'.

Stealing games

Stealing the keys

All you need for this game is a set of keys, a metal bowl, a blindfold, and a chair.

Put the keys in the metal bowl and place it under the chair.

The rest of the family makes a wide circle around the chair.

A person is blindfolded (the blind man) and sits in the chair, armed with a newspaper / foam sword / swim noodle.

The blind man must defend the keys; if he connects with someone, that person is either out or sent back to start again.

The objective is to sneak up, get the keys from the bowl, and get back to the starting area without being hit.

The successful sneaker gets to be the next blind man.

It can be played in turns or all at once, which makes for fast, competitive sneaking.

It can also be played in the dark.

Discuss strategies using questions like the following:

What did you do?

What worked well?

What didn't work?

What was the key to successful stealing? (See what I did there?)

The real steal

Each person involved in this game has to select an item of theirs to donate to the game, or you could buy enough small token gifts for the number of players involved. These items may potentially be stolen, so players need to be prepared for that when they choose their donations. All items must be wrapped in paper, and all players sit in a circle with their wrapped item in front of them.

Put a timer on for four to five minutes (less if there are not many people playing), and during that time, take turns throwing a die. Anyone who throws a six can take an item from someone else and add it to their own pile.

Once the timer finishes, everyone with one or more items in front of them gets to unwrap them and place them back down for everyone to see.

The timer will start again for three minutes, and this time anyone who rolls a six gets to choose an item to steal that they would like for themselves. This time you can see which are the best gifts to steal. There is no limit to how many times an item can be stolen within the allotted time.

At the end of the timer any items that remain in front of you are yours to keep!

- How did you feel when someone stole your item?
- How did you feel when you stole someone else's item?
- Did it make a difference if it was something you or the other person really wanted to keep?
- Was it fair that some people could end up with no items and others with lots?
- Was it fair that anyone could choose any item they wanted?
- Is stealing ever fair?

Nature thieves

In nature, there are examples of organisms that take things from one another, but it is not always a bad thing. This relationship between the organisms is called 'symbiosis', and in each relationship, at least one of the organisms benefits in some way. There are three types of symbiotic relationships:

Mutualism – both organisms benefit

Commensalism – one organism benefits, but the other is neither helped nor harmed

Parasitism – one organism is helped, but the other is harmed

Talk about the following with your child:

How might the environment be different without symbiosis?

Is it possible that parasitism is beneficial to the overall environment even though it harms an organism?

Do we, as humans, have a symbiotic relationship with any other organisms? How would you categorise them?

Cut the following cards apart and sort them into the three types of relationships.

Orchids are flowering plants that grow on trunks and branches of other trees and depend on the host plant for sunlight and nutrients that flow on the branches. They do not harm or help the host.

The egret is a type of heron that moves along with cattle or horses. They feed on insects that are stirred up when the animals feed. When they are not eating, they hop on their backs for a ride. They are light birds and do not limit the movement of the animals.

Intestinal flagellated protozoans digest the wood that is ingested by termites. The termites cannot digest the wood themselves, and the flagellated protozoans survive off the food ingested by the termites.

The remora, or suckerfish forms a relationship with large sea organisms. It has suckers that attach the fins of a host animal which helps them with transportation and protects them. The size of the remora makes it less intrusive and the host barely feels its presence.

Yucca moths lays her eggs in the seedpods of the yucca plant. The larvae hatch and feed on some, but not all of the seeds, then the moth pollinates the plants so that they can grow.

The tsetse fly is a biting fly that lives by feeding on the blood of vertebrate animals. Tsetse flies also transmit disease when they move from one organism to another.

Acacia ants live in a flower called the bullhorn acacia. The flower provides the ants with food and shelter and the ants drive away animals that may try to eat the flower.

Mosquitoes are small insects that feed on the blood of their host by piercing the skin to extract the protein and iron-rich blood. Their saliva is transferred to the host, causing an itchy rash.

The pea crab is a small crustacean that lives in oysters, sea urchins, or mollusks. They depend on their host for food, safety, and oxygen. Their feeding process can harm their host because they feed on the part of the animal that helps to carry food to their mouth.

Lessons to support learning

The demodex is a very small mite that lives in or near the hair follicles of dogs. They don't cause any symptoms for the dog.

The monarch butterfly attaches to milkweed during its larval stage as protection because the milkweed contains a toxic chemical that is harmful to most animals. The butterflies extract and store the toxin making them distasteful to birds. The larvae do not harm the plant.

A group of plants called dodder form masses of yellow, leafless vines over their hosts. They are aggressive plants and use root-like organs to steal water and nutrients from the host plant, often causing the host to die.

Clownfish live in sea anemones in the ocean. The sea anemones provide protection and shelter for the clownfish, and the clownfish cleans the sea anemone.

Army ants and birds have an interesting relationship. Birds trail army ants, not to feed on them, but to feed on the insects that are escaping the ants. The birds get their prey, but the ants are unaffected.

Bumblebees get nectar from flowers which they use to make their food. In moving from flower to flower to get nectar, the bees pollinate the flowers.

The oxpecker bird survives by eating parasites off of rhinos. The oxpecker makes a shrill noise when there is danger, alerting the rhino to the danger.

Ticks often attach themselves to dogs or cats by inserting their mouthparts into their skin. They feed on the blood of the dog or cat, which makes their skin become red and irritated and they can cause diseases.

Barnacles are crustaceans that cannot move on their own. They attach to whales during their larval stage where they grow and develop. They feed on plankton and other food while the whales move, but they do not feed on the blood or flesh of the whale, so the whales are not even aware of their presence.

4. LESSONS ABOUT OUR WORLD

LESSON 9 BIG QUESTION – WHAT IS A HERO?

Idea One:
A hero is someone you admire

Idea Two:
I admire my friend's super neat handwriting but she is not my hero

Dinner table conversations

Concept: Heroes

Main question: What is a hero?

Follow-up questions:

- What do heroes do?
- Can animals be heroes?
- Are heroes only in books and films?
- Do heroes always have super powers?
- Are heroes always brave?
- Do heroes have to be strong?
- Are all heroes famous?
- Are heroes real people?
- Do heroes have to be alive?
- Do you need a special outfit to be a hero?
- Do heroes always win against the odds?

Concept: Heroes

Main question: What makes someone a hero?

Follow-up questions:

- Are you a hero because of what you do or what you say?
- What things can you not do and still be a hero?
- When is it possible for a child to be a hero?
- What is the difference between male and female heroes?
- What should a hero look like?
- Are you born a hero, or do you become one?
- If you think someone is a hero, does that make them one?
- What is the difference between heroism and bravery?

Concept: Heroes

Main question: Is it possible for heroes to fail?

Follow-up questions:

- How much can a hero fail and still be a hero?
- Can you be a hero without taking risks?
- Should heroes be perfect?
- Does knowing failure make someone a true hero?
- If heroes do not experience failure, do they ever learn or develop new abilities?
- If heroes never experience failure, can they really experience success?
- How might flawed heroes be better role models than perfect heroes?
- How real is a perfect hero?
- How important are the flaws of our heroes in making them human and relatable?

Concept: Heroes

Main question: Are heroes important?

Follow-up questions:

- Why do you think so many people have a hero?
- Do you think having a hero is a positive thing?
- What if there were no heroes in the world?
- Is the word 'hero' used too often?
- How would meeting your hero affect you?
- Would you like to be a hero?
- Can heroes have a negative influence on us?
- Which types of heroes are the most important?
- Why might we have different heroes than other people?
- What is the difference between a hero and a role model?
- Should heroes get rewards?

Picture book activity

You can download activities for the book *Frog is a Hero* by Max Velthujjs on the Challenging Learning website:

www.challenginglearning.com/product/picture-books-frog-is-a-hero/

www.youtube.com/watch?v=RICdc7hHz6g

In addition to the questions on the activity download, you can use the following for discussion:

- Who do you think is more of a hero – Frog or Rat? Could either one of them have been the hero without the other one?

- How did Frog show bravery in his quest to get food? Can you be brave and afraid at the same time?

- Can you think about a time when you were really brave? Were you also afraid? What helped you to be brave? Would you do that again? What would you do differently?

Personal superpowers

Talk about superheroes and their superpowers. Ask your children what superpower they would have if they could have ANY superpower possible. Talk about why they would want that super-power and what they would do with it. Ask them how their superpower might help others. Discuss whether they would always want to have that superpower or if they would want to be able to turn it on and off.

Work with your child to decide what each of your real-life superpowers are. What are you really good at, passionate about, dedicated to, etc. Make a list of each of your superpowers. Talk about which ones are similar and which ones may complement each other. Discuss which ones you use the most and talk about why.

Make a commitment to use your superpower at least once during the week to help someone else or to improve something in your home, and write a journal or draw a picture about how it made you feel.

Superhero writing prompts

Choose from the following writing prompts this week:

- Pretend you're a superhero. Write a story about how you save the world from . . . *(you fill in the blank)*.

- Who is your favourite superhero and why? What qualities does this superhero have that you admire?

- Write a superhero story using at least five of the following words: brave, crash, defend, hero, mastermind, powers, sploosh, sidekick, villain, whoosh.

- You've just been given the ability to run extremely fast. Describe what it looks, feels, and sounds like to run at super-fast speeds.

- Write a funny story about a superhero who can't stop singing.

Superpower science

Have some fun with the scientific method by framing this experiment as a superpower exploration. Explain to your child/ren that Mr Freeze has been up to his naughty tricks and has frozen some toys in ice, and they need to become a superhero to rescue the toys. Tell them that you are going to use science to decide on the best superpower.

Supplies

Small plastic toys or coins

Small cups or an ice cube tray (if the toys or coins fit in the ice cube sections)

Water

Freezer

Squirt bottles

Substances that may be able to melt ice (salt, sugar, oil, vinegar, etc.; let your child brainstorm these)

Directions

- A day or two before you do the experiment, put the small toys in the ice cube trays or small cups with water and then freeze them.

- Show your child the items that are frozen in ice and ask them how they can save them.

- Ask your child what they notice and what they are thinking.

- Use the scientific method to set up an experiment for this heroic act:

  1 **Observe and question** – Have your child describe what they see and feel, then ask how they could save the toy/coin.

  2 **Background research** – Ask your child what they know about melting ice. When have they seen ice melted? What experience do they have with melting ice? Where could we find out more about melting ice?

  3 **Hypothesis** – Based on your discussion and research, decide on a few 'superpower' substances that might be helpful in melting the ice. Explain to your child that you will put these substances in a squirt bottle or a small bowl that you can pour over the ice, and then you will see which 'superpower' works the best for saving the toys/coins. Ask your child to make a hypothesis about which substances they think will work the best and then write them down.

  4 **Test/Experiment** – If using ice cubes, put the ice cubes in individual bowls. Place all of the cups/bowls on a table or counter, and pour each substance over the cups / ice cubes. Observe and record which substance(s) melted the ice the fastest. Consider setting a timer and noting how long it takes for each substance to melt the ice.

  5 **Draw conclusions** – Talk about what you observed and compare to your hypothesis.

  6 **Analyse your conclusions** – Ask your child how this information might be useful (for example, we use salt to melt ice on roads and walkways). Ask your child if they can think of other situations when we may want to be able to melt ice.

Community heroes

Brainstorm real-life heroes. Ask your child who they think are heroes. Talk about why they are heroes, whether they are always heroes, etc. Ask questions like the following:

- If someone is doing their job, are they still a hero?

- Can you be a hero if you are not saving people?

- Do you have to be brave to be a hero?

- Do you have to take risks to be a hero?

- Do people know when they are a hero?

Think about heroes in your community. Explore how you could send a hero in your community a thank you card or a picture. Talk with your child about how you will get it to them, and then follow through by delivering/sending the thank you.

Zero the hero maths game

The goal of the game is to end up exactly at zero.

- Sit in a circle or around a table. Each person starts with 20 objects (buttons, noodles, pebbles, etc.)

- The youngest person goes first by rolling a six-sided die. Whatever number they roll, they take away that many objects from their pile of 20 objects, and they put them in the middle. Each person gets a turn to roll the die and subtract from 20.

- Continue working around the circle with each person rolling the die and subtracting from their pile.

- If someone gets close to zero and does not have enough objects to subtract the number that is rolled, they have to take that many objects from the centre.

- The winner ends up at exactly zero and calls out 'ZERO THE HERO!'

Variations

- For older children, do not use objects, but rather write the numbers and use mental maths to subtract and add.

- For a twist (and to make the game much longer) – if someone can't subtract the number they roll, they have to take all of the objects that are in the centre.

- Another twist – if someone can't subtract the number they roll, they have to take that number of objects from someone else in the game.

Personal heroes

Tell your child about someone in your life who has been a hero to you. Explain why they are your hero, what you admire about them, and how they have impacted your life. Share any pictures, stories, or artefacts that you have.

Ask your child if they have anyone in their life that they consider a hero. Ask why that person is a hero, how the person has helped them, and what qualities make the person a hero.

Talk about how sometimes heroes are like mentors who encourage us and cheer us on. Work with your child to write goals for yourselves to become personal heroes for others. Write them down and put them somewhere as a reminder to BE A HERO!

Defining a hero using an opinion line

Here you can use an opinion line with quotes about heroes to develop your child's concept about what a hero is.

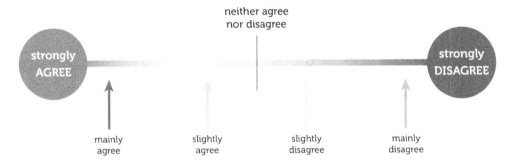

Start out by asking your child what they think a hero is. Jot down their ideas and come up with a definition of a hero together. Write it down and set it aside.

Now share the following quotes (you can cut them into strips so that your child can physically place them in a line) about heroes and ask your child to place them on an opinion line that ranges from 'strongly agree' to 'strongly disagree'. As they place the quotes, ask questions like these:

- Why do you only agree with this rather than strongly agree with it?
- What is it about this one that makes you feel strongly about it?
- If you only disagree with this rather than strongly disagree with it, does that mean that there is a small part of it that you agree with?
- What would you change about the one you disagree with to make you agree with it?
- What would you need to change about the one you agree with to make you strongly agree with it?
- Would you change your definition of a hero after doing this activity? How?

'I think a hero is really any person intent on making this a better place for all people.'

– Maya Angelou[1]

'It doesn't take a hero to order men into battle. It takes a hero to be one of those men who goes into battle.'

– Norman Schwarzkopf[2]

'A hero is someone who has given his or her life to something bigger than oneself.'

– Joseph Campbell

'I think a hero is someone who understands the degree of responsibility that comes with his freedom.'

– Bob Dylan[3]

'A hero is brave in deeds as well as words.'

– Aesop's Fables ('The Hunter and the Woodsman')[4]

(More quotes can be found at https://inspiremykids.com/great-hero-quotes-for-kids/.)

Follow-up research

Challenge your child to research some of the authors of the quotes and talk about whether they are heroes themselves or if they have experienced something that makes them knowledgeable about heroes. Talk about whether people who have first-hand experience with heroes or heroic acts have a better understanding of what it means to be a hero.

Ranking heroic acts

Talk to your child about heroic acts. Brainstorm some examples of heroic acts and decide on a description of a heroic act. Then cut out the following cards and have your child arrange them into a diamond four (for younger children) or a diamond nine, placing the most heroic acts at the top and the least heroic acts at the bottom. Since they will not use all of the cards, you can repeat the process by eliminating some cards or choosing some cards that must be used.

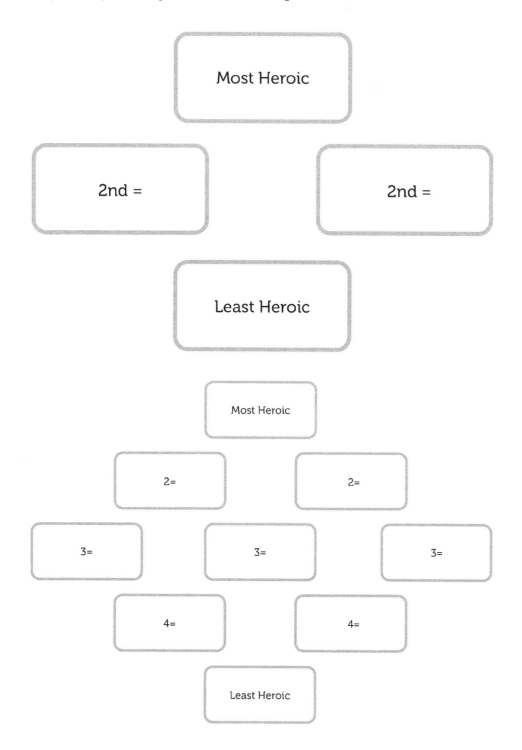

Killing a spider that is in your home	Saving a baby bird that falls out of a nest	A fireman pulling a dog from a burning house	A doctor performing a life-saving surgery
Building a house for a homeless family	Running away from two classmates who are fighting	Planting trees	Learning self-defence
Running a marathon	Asking for help when you are confused at school	Holding your younger sibling's hand when crossing the street	Wearing a helmet when you ride your bicycle

Hero antonyms

Work with your child to come up with a list of qualities or characteristics of heroes like 'brave', 'strong', 'caring', etc. Write the words down on a piece of paper or whiteboard.

Talk to your children about antonyms and explain that they are words that are the opposite of another word. Go through your list and see if you can come up with antonyms for each of the qualities/characteristics you came up with.

Ask your child if heroes might have both qualities. Work with your child to come up with possible scenarios, for example, a hero who is brave in some ways but fearful in others.

Concept target

Together with your child/ren, create a list of vocabulary related to the concept of hero.

Here is a list of related vocabulary to start you off using the concept target. It would be great if you and your child could add to this list or make your own list. Remember to draw on your discussions from some of the other activities to help to evaluate each word or term.

- Brave
- Superpower
- Risks
- Heroic
- Saving lives
- Strength
- Battle
- Selfless

Heroes

Superhero powers in the animal world

Talk about superhero powers with your child/ren. What powers can they name? What makes these powers special?

Introduce the following cards by talking about the superpower that each of the creatures possesses. Encourage your child to rank the animals according to which one they feel has the greatest 'superpower'. They can do this in a diamond formation (like the diamond ranking in the heroic acts activity) with the greatest superpower at the top, the one they feel is the least impressive at the bottom, and the others in between. Can you find pictures to go with the descriptions of these creatures? Can you find any other creatures in the animal world with superpowers? Which of these superpowers would you choose for yourself?

The Jellyfish

Superpower: Immortality

The Turritopsis nutricula as it has the ability to revert back to its immature, young state after it mates. The jellyfish sinks down to the ocean floor in this immature state and begins the process of growing to maturity again. As the process can be performed time and time again, the jellyfish is basically immortal and can live forever. Unless they get eaten of course.

©2020 www.challenginglearning.com

The Wood Frog

Superpower: Blood freezing

The wood frog hibernates by digging into frozen ground found in much of North America. To handle the extreme cold, the wood frog freezes its own blood. Wood frogs belong to a small group of animals that can freeze but not die. The wood frog buries itself and goes into deep hibernation. Its breathing and heartbeat stop, and as much as 65% of the water in its body turns to ice. For two or three months of each winter it is frozen, with a body temp between -1°C & -6°C. When spring arrives, the ice melts, heartbeat and breathing return, and the frog is as good as new!

©2020 www.challenginglearning.com

The Lyrebird

Superpower: Imitation

The Turritopsis nutricula as it has the ability to revert back to its immature, young state after it mates. The jellyfish sinks down to the ocean floor in this immature state and begins the process of growing to maturity again. As the process can be performed time and time again, the jellyfish is basically immortal and can live forever. Unless they get eaten of course.

©2020 www.challenginglearning.com

The Mimic Octopus

Superpower: Shape-shifting

The mimic octopus is able to change shape in a matter of seconds and can mimic the shape of a number of different ocean creatures. It has been known to change to the shape of a sea snake, a lion fish, a flat fish and a jelly fish. The fact that all of these fish are poisonous suggests that the mimic octopus changes shape as a defence mechanism, in order to stop predators attacking it.

The Chameleon

Superpower: Colour changing

Chameleons have the ability to be able to change the colour of their skin in a matter of minutes. One of the main reasons is to camouflage themselves with their surroundings in order to avoid predators. Another reason for this colour change is down to mood: chameleons will often change to a darker colour to show anger and try to intimidate others, while a lighter, multi-coloured shade is used in order to attract a mate.

The Basilisk Lizard

Superpower: Walking on water

These lizards can achieve this impressive trick thanks to their long toes, which have fringes of skin in between, that they rapidly slap against the water, creating air pockets and keeping them afloat. The basilisk lizard will always stay near water as they use their water-walking skills to escape predators.

The Dung Beetle

Superpower: Super strength

The dung beetle possesses super strength and has the ability to carry things many, many times larger/heavier than itself. It can pull up to 1,141 times its own body weight. It would be like a human being able to pull 6 double-decker buses filled with people. The Dung Beetle is, pound for pound, the most powerful creature in the animal kingdom.

The Alpine Ibex

Superpower: Gravity defying

The alpine ibex mountain goat can climb places that no other animal would even dare go near. These include dams, cliffs and mountain sides that are almost vertical. It has short legs and a very low centre of gravity. It also has extremely powerful muscles, especially in its back legs. Its hooves are designed with a thin, solid outer rim and a soft central area which makes them ideal for climbing.

The Peregrene Falcon

Superpower: Speed flying

Peregrine falcons are the fastest birds in existence. They've been clocked at speeds up to 240 miles per hour. That's faster than a 100 mph sneeze and around the same speed as a Formula 1 racing car. Peregrines are light in weight, aerodynamically shaped, and have strong respiratory (breathing) systems, all of which allows them to be the fastest birds of prey, and animals in general.

Create your own literary hero

Read through the information cards about the six different literary hero types. Talk about the key differences between each one and encourage your child/ren to think of examples from stories, comics, TV, or films to match each of the different hero types.

Ask your child/ren to choose a hero type to develop as a character of their own. Use the 'Character Profile' template to help them do this. Once the character is fully thought through and developed, write the character into a story. Remember to stay true to the type of hero you chose. It would be good to develop other hero characters to put into your story too. You could also draw a profile picture of each hero type and label them. Have fun!

Types of heroes in literature (stories)

Classical Hero

These are normal people with a great talent or quality that makes them stand out from the crowd. This might be courage, or strength or a skill such as magic. We feel admiration and wonder for this character.

Tragic Hero

This is a person with heroic qualities who also has a flaw or weakness in their character. They are doomed by fate to suffer and fail despite putting up a great struggle. We can feel pity and fear for this character.

Superhero

These characters often start out as normal people and something happens that causes them to acquire a power to make them 'super'. Other superheroes are born with superhuman qualities. We are amazed and wowed by these characters.

Everyman Hero

In stories 'everyman' is the term we use to mean an ordinary, everyday person who the reader can easily identify with. They have no outstanding qualities, abilities or powers. They are placed in circumstances where they have to act with heroic qualities such as courage or selflessness against all the odds. We respect and honour these characters.

Epic Hero

These are usually heroes of a tragedy. They are legendary and their heroism is so awe inspiring that it is told in tales for hundreds of years. An epic hero wins his or her own fortune through their heroic acts and deeds. They often face larger than life challenges and can be great warriors, kings, queens, demi-gods or knights. These characters excite us and engage us in their stories.

Anti Hero

These are characters who lack all the usual characteristics of heroes. Some may even appear to act more like villains. They may be dishonest, spiteful and rebellious. We don't always like these characters to begin with. However, there are two sides to these characters and we slowly begin to see their good qualities too. Sometimes these characters begin as good people but have unlikable qualities or they can begin as a really horrible character who has a kind heart. We can feel confused about whether we like these characters or not.

Hero character profile

First Impression	**Likes & dislikes**
Name:	Family:
Age:	Friends:
Appearance/looks:	Enemies:
Job/background:	Love:
	Favourite things:
First introduction of the hero to the reader: *(How do we meet this character?)*	Dislikes:
Journey/storyline	**Personality**
Goal/aim: *(What character wantd or needs to do?)*	Flaws/weaknesses:
Motivation: *(Why they want or need to do it?)*	Attitudes/behaviours:
Conflict: *(What gets in their way?)*	Abilities/skills:
Change hero goes through:	Beliefs:

What is the difference between a hero and a villain?

Brave	Good	Loyal	Ambitious
Interesting	Likeable	Evil	Sneaky
Honest	Selfless	Cruel	Clever
Liar	Determined	Proud	Kind
Persuasive	Good leader	Protective	Destructive
Caring	Rule breaker	Selfish	Resilient
Flexible	Fearless	Strong	Thoughtful
Powerful	Sad	Happy	Funny

Use the characteristics listed here and the Venn diagram template to compare the similarities and differences between heroes and villains. You can cut each characteristic out, and your child/ren can place them in the part of the diagram that they think they should go into. If there are any characteristics that do not apply to heroes or villains, they should go outside of the diagram.

Challenge your child's thinking and reasoning as they make their choices.

- Would that only apply to heroes/villains?
- Can you think of an example of a hero or villain with this characteristic?
- Is someone still a hero if they have some negative characteristics?
- Is someone still a villain if they have positive characteristics?

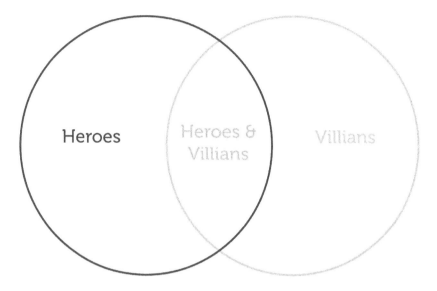

LESSON 10 BIG QUESTION – WHAT IS LANGUAGE?

Idea One:
Language is used to understand others

Idea Two:
My dog understands me but doesn't have language

Language

STRONGER LEARNING for STRONGER LIVES

Dinner table conversations

Concept: Language

Main question: What is language?

Follow-up questions:

- What is the difference between language and communication?
- Does language always have to be spoken?
- When did language begin?
- How do we learn language?
- Is all language learned?
- Are there languages that do not have words?
- Are babies born with language?
- Do animals have a language?
- Is language mankind's greatest invention?
- Is there such a thing as natural language?
- What is the difference between artificial and human language?

Concept: Language

Main question: How important is language?

Follow-up questions:

- Can we communicate without a language?
- What would happen if we had no language at all?
- Why do we need language?
- How important is it that we share the names and labels for things?
- How important is it that we understand each other?
- What role does language play in the relationships we develop with others?
- What is the relationship between language and power?
- How important is it that public speakers use clear language?
- Why is language important to culture?
- Can a community or society exist without language?

Concept: Language

Main question: What is the connection between language and thinking?

Follow-up questions:

- Does language always communicate our thoughts?
- How could language get in the way of your thoughts?
- Can we understand other people's thoughts through their use of language?
- Does our language influence how we think, or does how we think influence our language?
- Do we think using personal images, or do we think using a shared language?
- Do you dream in a language?
- How might you express feelings if you had no language?
- Do we think in words or pictures?

Concept: Language

Main question: Is language the key to successful learning?

Follow-up questions:

- Can language be misleading?
- How important are words in helping us to understand the nature of things?
- Does language allow us to gain knowledge?
- How much does language influence people?
- Are the images in your head for things the same as everyone else's?
- Can you learn without language?
- If someone argues that the grass is blue, does that make it true?
- Does language encourage independent thought and opinion or discourage it?
- What is the difference between our meaning of language and our use of it?
- What is the role of language in the sharing of common ideas?

Picture book activity

Same, Same but Different by Jenny Sue Kostecki-Shaw is a book about two boys who are pen pals and live in different parts of the world. They discover that even though they live in very different places, they have a lot of things in common.

YouTube version: www.youtube.com/watch?v=ze11Q-S8-LA

Use questions like the following to discuss the story:

- Would the boys speak the same language?
- How did the boys communicate?
- What do they mean by same, but different?
- How are you the same as the boys in the book?
- Can you think of some ways that you might be the same as kids from another country, but different?

Have your child make a collage or book that they could use to communicate with a pen pal who speaks a different language. Talk about the following:

- What should you include?
- What would you like to know about your pen pal?
- What is unique about you? What could you share that is special about where you live?

Body language

Talk about how we communicate with body language. We use body language to communicate how we feel. Sometimes it is conscious, but often we do not think about the messages we send with our body language.

Demonstrate body language, like slouching in your seat, turning your body away, or putting your head on the table, and have your child guess how you are feeling. Next, have your child use body language to express feelings so that you can guess.

When you read a story, have your children act out with their body language how the characters are feeling or reacting.

Signs and symbols

Talk about some of the things you have to say a lot during the day, for example, 'wash your hands' or 'pick up your toys'. Decide on a hand symbol that you can use instead, or design a sign that you can just point to. Try to only use that symbol or sign for the whole week.

Add more signs and symbols as you notice phrases or questions that are repeated.

Nonsense poems

Nonsense poetry is often our first introduction to poetry, read to us in the form of nursery rhymes when we are young. Nonsense poetry has been passed down through many generations and is as old as language itself.

Nonsense poems are poems that intentionally don't make a lot of sense. Some use made-up words, while others contradict themselves or use language in random or unusual ways. At their heart, nonsense rhymes are playful and intended to be humorous and puzzling. Some poems use made-up words to describe things or just to make a nice sound. Lewis Carroll, Edward Lear, and Spike Milligan are good authors to read if you like nonsense poetry.

In the nonsense poem 'On the Ning Nang Nong' by Spike Milligan (which can be found online), there are lots of examples of onomatopoeia (words that make the sound of thing they are describing). Examples of these words can be found in almost every line, such as 'and the monkeys all say BOO!' in line three. Another great example within the text is 'jibber jabber joo'.

The poet plays with the sounds and the meanings of the language in this poem. He uses a combination of real words and made-up nonsense words. Some words that are familiar to us include 'clang' and 'ping'. These are real words that have an onomatopoeic meaning or a sound we recognise. Some of the nonsense words include 'Nong' and 'Nang'. These do not have any meaning, and it is up to the reader to make their own meaning of them or to just enjoy them for their sounds.

Challenge your child/ren to create their own nonsense poems. They can play around with familiar language, sounds, rhymes, and rhythm. It would also be fun to make up some language of their own in the form of nonsense words and use these within their poems. Have fun and be creative!

Learn to count in four languages

You can use the YouTube video found at www.youtube.com/watch?v=uTsFBOIoLxY to learn a song for counting in English, Spanish, French, and Japanese.

Talk about how the numbers are similar and different, and ask your children what they notice about them.

English

one

two

three

four

five

six

seven

eight

nine

ten

Spanish

    uno (oo-no)

    dos (dose)

    tres (tress)

    cuatro (kwah-tro)

    cinco (sink-oh)

    sies (sayss)

    siete (syet-tay)

    ocho (oh-cho)

    nueve (nwehv-eh)

    diez (dyess)

French

    un (ahn)

    deux (deuh)

    trois (twah)

    quatre (katr)

    cinq (sank)

    six (seese)

    sept (set)

    huit (wheet)

    neuf (nurf)

    dix (deese)

Japanese

    ichi (each)

    ni (knee)

    san (sahn)

    shi (she)

    go (goh)

    roku (loh-koo)

    shichi (she-tchee)

    hachi (ha-tchi)

    kyuu (kyoo)

    juu (joo)

Language of art

Expressive arts and design is great way to develop a child's imagination and creativity. The use of media provides a language to help children to represent and understand their own feelings and ideas. Help your child create a 'language of life' collage.

You will need the following materials:

- Old magazines, newspapers, picture books, and scrap paper
- Coloured pens and pencils
- Scissors and glue
- Cardboard or thick paper to create the collage on

This activity aims to give children a way to explore their values and what is important to them and express these through their own language. Ask your child/ren what makes them feel good about their own and other people's behaviour. Explain that the behaviours and attitudes that we think are important and make us happy are called our 'values'. Encourage your child to question these values and generate associated language to go with them. Ideas to investigate include honesty, respect, caring for others, determination, love, independence, teamwork, etc.

Once your child/ren have come up with the words to represent the values they hold dear, encourage them to begin selecting images, words, phrases, or colours from the magazines and newspapers. They should use these to create a collage that they feel reflects their language to live by. This can be picture based or abstract; it's all about how their words make them feel. They can display their collage to remind them of their core values.

Sign language

Talk about all of the reasons that people may use sign language. Sign language is helpful for people who cannot hear but also for people who are non-verbal. Sometimes young children are able to learn some simple signs before they are able to speak. Have a dialogue with your child about sign language using questions like the following:

- What do you know about sign language? Are there signs for letters, words, phrases?
- What are some of the advantages to using sign language?
- How do you think people learn sign language?
- Just like we speak different languages, do you think there are also different versions of sign language?

There are actually more than 130 versions of sign language with new ones still being created. There are two versions of a sign language alphabet presented here. One is British and the other is American. Compare the two alphabets and talk about how they are similar and different. Decide whether or not someone who knows American Sign Language would understand someone who is using British Sign Language and vice versa.

Work with your child/ren to learn their names in sign language (using one or both versions), and have them practice until they can do it from memory.

Lessons to support learning

British Sign Language

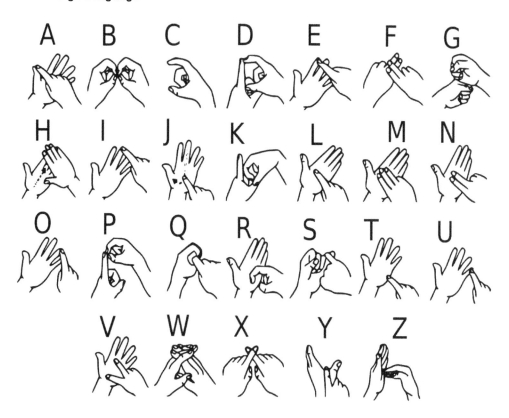

American Sign Language

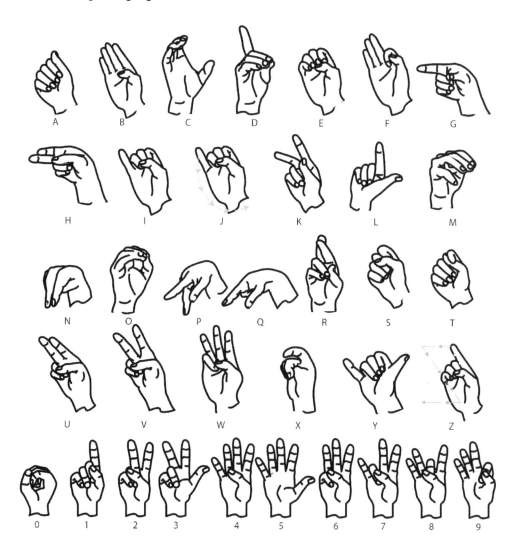

Code language

Create your own code language by assigning a symbol, shape, or number to each letter of the alphabet. This becomes your code language key.

Then create secret messages using the code that you created. Leave notes for your child and have them decode them using the key that you created.

See if your child can respond to you using the code you created.

Descriptive language scavenger hunt

The goal is to find objects in the house that are named for exactly what they do, for example, a toothbrush – you use it to brush your teeth.

- Set a timer for ten minutes.
- Send everyone in the house to find as many objects as they can.
- Come back together and present your objects.
- Each person presents their object and explains how the name of the object tells what it does.

Whoever finds the most wins and gets to decide who has to put everything away. ☺

Change the game by finding objects that are NOT named for what they do, and then when you come back to present your objects, you have to make up a name for the object that DOES say what it does.

Animal language

Animals can't talk, but they do have a way to communicate with each other. Talk about the different ways that animals communicate.

- How do they communicate (ask about specific animals)? What sounds do they make, or what actions do they engage in to communicate?
- What types of communication do you think they have?
- Do you think all animals communicate? Do you think animals only communicate with the same kinds of animals?
- Do animals communicate with humans?

Write or tell a story or draw a comic about your favourite animal or pet suddenly being able speak a language that only the two of you know and understand.

- What would you talk about?
- Would you want others to know about it?
- What would the language involve? Would it be sounds, words, non-verbal, etc.?

Non-verbal language

Refer to the strategy guide for information about sorting and classifying and Venn diagrams.

We can communicate a great deal without ever saying a word. This is called 'non-verbal communication', and the language we use for this includes facial expressions, body language, sitting posture and position, and eye contact.

It is tricky to always get this language correct, but it is a very important language to learn.

It allows you to show agreement/disagreement; to give someone who is talking confidence, reassurance, and encouragement; and to show that you are interested and listening to what someone has to say.

Making eye contact with the speaker	Nodding head	Smiling	Looking at the ground	Yawning
Smirking	Giggling	Tilting your head to the side	Crossing your arms across your chest	Tapping your fingers
Playing with your hair	Picking your nose	Thumbs up	Open arms	Shedding tears
Frowning	Rubbing eyes	Head in hands	Shaking head from side to side	Thumbs down

Sort the non-verbal language cards into two sets: 'positive non-verbal language' and 'negative non-verbal language'. Are there any cards that could go in the centre because they can be positive and negative? Why do you think this is?

Now try placing all the cards along a line with 'always positive' at one end and 'always negative' at the other.

- Are there any cards that can go at the very end points?

- Which card goes bang in the middle?

- What makes some more positive or more negative than others?

You can also use these cards to do diamond ranking, which is described in the introduction.

Language of numbers

Play a game of 'what's my number?' with your child/ren. Write a number on a piece of paper without anyone seeing, fold the paper in half to keep the number secret, and place it in front of you.

Your child/ren have to ask a number of questions using mathematical language/vocabulary to try and work out the identity of the hidden number. You can only answer yes or no. They should be discouraged from guessing by giving them three lives (guesses) only and 20 questions. Using a whiteboard, flipchart, or large piece of paper, record the questions that get positive answers, for example, if they ask if the number is even and the answer is yes, then you would write 'even' on the paper. This will build up a profile of the hidden number.

Encourage your child to use the following mathematical language to ask their questions:

- Odd/Even

- Multiple of x / In the x times table

- One-digit / Two-digit / Three-digit / Four-digit number

- Prime number

- Square number

- Factor of / Can divide into x

- Greater than / Less than

- In the range of *x* to *y*

- Negative number / Positive number

- Whole number / Decimal number

- Is the hundreds/tens/units digit a 5?

It is important to keep the activity fun and engaging. Your child/ren may not be familiar with all of this language yet, and it is important that they access the activity at their level and that you choose numbers within their capability range. We want to challenge them by not making it too easy (this would be a dull game), but if it is too difficult, it will make the game unpleasant and stressful.

When your child/ren use questions that do not include mathematical language, be positive and encouraging and reinforce the correct vocabulary. For example:

Child: Does it have two numbers in it?

Parent: Good question! You mean is it a two-digit number, yes it is! Well done.

Turn the tables and get your child to choose the hidden number and challenge you to work out what it is.

Another challenge, as well as increasing the complexity of the number, is to reduce the number of questions and lives your child/ren are allowed.

Concept target

Together with your child/ren, create a list of vocabulary related to the concept of language.

Here is a list of related vocabulary to start you off using the concept target. It would be great if you and your child could add to this list or make your own list. Remember to draw on your discussions from some of the other activities to help to evaluate each word or term.

- Communication

- Words

- Talking

- Symbols

- Signs

- Action

- Sound

- Understanding

Telephone game

If you have enough people in the family, play the telephone game. You sit in a circle, and one person whispers a message into the ear of the person next to them, then that person whispers the message to the next person, and so on until the person who starts the message hears the message. Talk about what happened to the message.

- Was the final message the same as the original one? What happened?
- What can happen when we hear something and then repeat it to someone else? When might this be a problem?
- Is it considered gossiping or untruthful if we just did not hear it right and then told someone else?
- How can we make sure that we get someone's message correct?

Forbidden words game

Use the cards that follow to play the game forbidden words. See how many of the words you can get your child to guess – or, for older children, how many of the words your child can get you to guess. You or your child have to describe the word at the top of the card; however, the words listed below it are 'forbidden' and cannot be used.

Now make your own forbidden words cards.

- How will you decide which words are 'forbidden'?
- Would other people think of different words to be 'forbidden'?
- Are some words harder than others to think of 'forbidden' words for?

Forbidden words game cards

Park	Car	Dog
• Play	• Drive	• Pet
• Swings	• Wheels	• Bark
• Slides	• Garage	• Tail
• Trees	• Steer	• Fur

©2020 www.challenginglearning.com   ©2020 www.challenginglearning.com   ©2020 www.challenginglearning.com

Sleep

- Night
- Nap
- Bed
- Rest

Home

- Live
- Family
- Address
- Room

Eat

- Breakfast
- Lunch
- Dinner
- Food

Game

- Play
- Winner
- Loser
- Board

Read

- Book
- Bed
- Story
- Words

Tree

- Leaves
- Trunk
- Roots
- Shade

Ball

- Round
- Bounce
- Throw
- Roll

Cloud

- Sky
- Rain
- Fluffy
- White

Dance

- Music
- Spin
- Twirl
- Party

Lessons to support learning

Face

- Eyes
- Nose
- Mouth
- Head

Phone

- Talk
- Call
- Cell
- Text

School

- Learn
- Class
- Teacher
- Grade

Smile

- Happy
- Mouth
- Frown
- Teeth

Cake

- Birthday
- Frosting
- Candles
- Decorate

Bug

- Spider
- Fly
- Lady
- Ant

Friend

- Best
- Pal
- Mate
- Play

Chair

- Sit
- Table
- Sofa
- Rocking

Language of emotions

Support your child/ren to create a mood circle. Explain that we all have a full range of emotions. Sometimes they can feel very big, and we can find them difficult to understand and deal with. Sometimes they can be small, and we may not even recognise them. As we are growing and developing, our reactions and feelings about things go through many changes. We may feel sad and slow one moment and then energetic and lively the next. At times we may be confused by our moods and find it difficult to find the language to describe how we are feeling. This is normal, and creating and using a mood circle can help us to build the emotional language that will communicate our feelings and moods in a more constructive way.

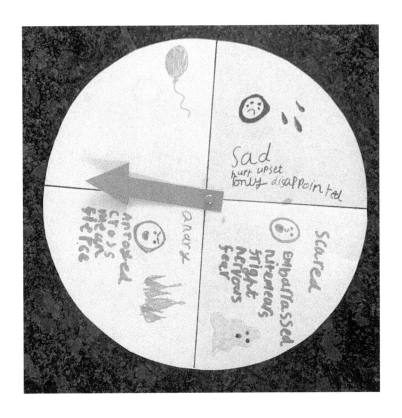

- Using a paper plate or a circle of card, divide it into four or eight sections depending on how many moods you want to focus on.

- Draw faces or create your own emojis with different moods/emotions for each section.

- Think of different words that relate to that mood and write them in the same section. For example, on the section with a happy face you could write 'excited', 'cheerful', 'energetic', 'hopeful', 'creative', 'amused', etc. Relating to a sad face, you could add 'lonely', 'bored', 'tired', 'guilty', 'embarrassed', 'sick', etc.

- Cut out a little arrow and attach it with a fastener of some kind in the centre of the circle so that it can be rotated to point to the different mood sections.

If you're feeling fancy, you can take photos of your child acting out all the different types of moods and stick the pictures on the mood circle.

Discuss the mood circle together and review some of the language used and the feelings they relate to. Use the wheel as you talk with your child about their day and encourage them to use the language on the circle to explain how they felt during the experiences they share. The mood circle can be used as a way of opening up a family discussion about how each person's day has gone. This models the fact that experiencing different moods and emotions is a normal part of everyone's day, and it is a good opportunity to discuss different ways of dealing with difficult, uncomfortable, and negative emotions we may experience.

Other activities

Weather watch

Talk with your child about the outside temperature and which temperatures feel warm and which temperatures feel cool. Pick three times during the day to check the temperature. First go outside to feel the temperature, then check it online or on your phone. Keep a chart or a list of the temperatures

Have your child write down other observations that they think may impact the weather.

- Is it cloudy?
- Is it night-time?
- Is it raining?
- Is the wind blowing?

After a few days, have your child try to predict the temperature just by going outside.

Talk about how the outside temperature changes not only throughout the day, but also throughout the year. See if your child can explain why they think these changes happen.

Five frame / Ten frame, part 2

Use the five frame or ten frame that you created earlier and add another. If you have a preschooler, it is best to continue with a five frame, but if you have an early primary student, you can start with a ten frame.

- Review the number sentences you came up with earlier.
- Now add the second frame and talk about why you would need a second frame. Hopefully your child will share that you may need a second frame for numbers greater than 5 or 10. If not, use questioning or just put out a pile of buttons or counters that is higher than 5 or 10.
- Lay out combinations of buttons that total more than 5 or 10. For example, make a pile of four buttons and a pile of three buttons. Or, for the ten frame, lay out a pile of six buttons and a pile of seven buttons.
- Work with your child to fill one frame first, and then talk about what to do next – begin putting buttons in the second frame.
- Now talk about how you can count them. See if your child can come up with the fact that you can simply start with 5 or 10 rather than counting all of the buttons in that frame.
- Practice doing this with different combinations of buttons.
- You can also write the number sentences for the problems you create.

LESSON 11 BIG QUESTION – WHAT IS EXPLORATION?

Idea One:
Exploration can be very dangerous and risky

Idea Two:
There are risks in everything we do. We would never go anywhere or do anything if we didn't take risks.

Dinner table conversations

Concept: Exploration

Main question: What is exploration?

Follow-up questions:

- What is the difference between searching and exploring?
- If you know what you are looking for, are you searching or exploring?
- Does exploring always have to involve some kind of travel?
- Can you explore without ever leaving the house?
- How is exploration today different to exploration 600 years ago?
- What do we mean when we say we are 'exploring the meaning of life'?

Concept: Exploration

Main question: What makes someone an explorer?

Follow-up questions:

- Can anybody be an explorer?
- Do explorers always have to be brave?
- How old do you need to be before you can be an explorer?
- Is everyone who seeks new knowledge an explorer?

- Are all explorers adventure seekers?

- Can you be an explorer and not know you are one?

- Are famous explorers simply more successful than the non-famous ones?

- If you are a scientist, are you automatically an explorer?

Concept: Exploration

Main question: How dangerous is exploration?

Follow-up questions:

- How much is risk-taking an essential part of exploration?

- How much is the risk and danger element of exploration part of why people want to do it?

- If explorers are venturing into the unknown, how aware (or unaware) of the dangers of this exploration are they?

- Is the danger of exploration greater for the explorer or for the place, people, or things they are exploring?

- Do the positives of exploration always outweigh the negatives?

- Does exploring something or somewhere change it forever?

Concept: Exploration

Main question: How important is exploration?

Follow-up questions:

- What might the world look like today if nobody had ever explored?

- What should the key purpose of exploration be?

- Are some types of exploration more important than others?

- What is the most important benefit of exploration?

- What is the most important concern about exploration?

- Would we be able to enjoy the environment we do if exploration had not happened?

- How connected are exploration and learning? Can we have one without the other?

- Which types of exploration do you think should continue and which should stop?

Picture book activity

Morris Mole by Dan Yaccarino is a book about a little mole who decides to explore another option for finding food when his family is running out of food.

YouTube version: www.youtube.com/watch?v=-7HoXkY_r78

Use the following questions to discuss the book with your child:

- What did Morris discover on his exploration? Did he discover more than he set out to discover?

- Is it considered exploration if you are looking for something specific?

- What do you think Morris's family learned from his exploration? Do all explorations bring about new knowledge or ideas?

Treasure maps

One type of exploration that is present in many stories is exploring for treasures using a treasure map. Have some fun in your home with treasure maps. Hide a prize or a note somewhere in the house, and then draw a treasure map of the house to lead your child to the 'treasure'. Consider including some obstacles or tricks.

Once your child uses the map to find the 'treasure', have them hide something for you and create a treasure map. Encourage creativity and fun. Use questions like the following to have a dialogue about your experience:

- What was the hardest part about following the map that I made for you? What was the hardest part about making a map?

- What are some important things to include on a map?

- How do you think explorers knew where they were going long ago when we didn't have maps?

- Are there places in our current world that we could explore that might not have maps?

Grid exploration

Explorers often use maps with grids to track their movements or to make note of where they discover treasures or interesting artefacts. Tell your child that they are going to be like a real-life explorer to plot points on a graph and find a secret message about how to be an good explorer.

Use the exploration grid (Figure 17) to plot the points (to find where the letter and number intersect for D26, for example, go over to D and then up to 26) and connect them in the order they are listed using a ruler or straight edge. Each time you see the * symbol, it means that you start a new letter or shape. Note that sometimes you trace back over a line within a letter or shape.

*D26, D30, F30, F26, F28, D28; *G30, G26, I26; *J30, J26, K28, L26, L30; *M26, M30, O30, O26, O28, M28; *P30, P28, Q27, Q26, Q27, R28, R30; *U30, S30, S28, U28, U26, S26; *D18, F18, F17, E16, F15, F14, D14, D18; *I18, G18, G16, I16, G16, G14, I14; *D6, B6, B2, D2; *E6, E2, G2, G6; *H2, H6, J6, J4, I4, J2; *N2, N6, P6, P2, N2; *Q6, Q2, S2, S6; *V6, T6, T4, V4, V2, T2; *Q14, S14, S11, Q11, Q12, S12, Q12, Q13, S13, Q13, Q14, P15, P19, Q20, S20, T19, T15, S14; *P20, O21; *Q21, Q23; *S21, S23; *T20, U21

STEM exploration – space travel

Part 1 – History of space travel

In the 1960s, the United States and the Soviet Union engaged in what has been called the 'space race'. It was a competition to be the first country to go into space. The intent of both countries was to explore outer space to learn more about the Earth, but also to learn more about what lies beyond the Earth. As a result of this space race, on April 12, 1961, the Soviet Union became the first to put a man in space, but the United States was the first to put a man on the moon, on July 20, 1969. Share with your child the following events that have occurred throughout history in our efforts to explore space, and note the various vehicles (in bold) that were used for the exploration:

- October 4, 1957 – The first **satellite, Sputnik 1**, was launched into orbit around the Earth.

- April 12, 1961 – Yuri Gagarin was the first man to travel into space and orbit the Earth in a **Vostok 1 space capsule powered by the Vostok 3KA spacecraft**.

- September 12, 1962 – John F. Kennedy delivered a speech in which he announced his goal to put a man on the moon by the end of the decade.

- December 21, 1968 – Frank Borman, James Lovell, and William Anders were the first humans to orbit the Earth in the **Apollo 8 Spacecraft powered by the Saturn V rocket**.

- July 20, 1969 – Neil Armstrong stepped off of the **lunar module Eagle** to step on the moon.

- November 17, 1970 – The first **remote-controlled robot, the Lunokhod 1** explored the moon.

- April 19, 1971 – The first space station, **Salyut 1** was launched; the first crew arrived on June 7, 1971.

- May 30, 1971 – The **satellite Mariner 9** became the first artificial satellite of Mars.

- July 31, 1971 – The first human-driven **Lunar Roving Vehicle** (or moon buggy) was used to explore the moon.

- July 4, 1997 – A **small rover called Sojourner** became the first wheeled Mars exploration vehicle.

If your child shows a lot of interest, you can also view a read-aloud of the book *Moonshot* by Brian Floca here: www.youtube.com/watch?v=o2ApgcRQ7tk.

Part 2 – Design your own space vehicle

Design and build your own spaceship, space station, or satellite. What features will you add to make your creation safe as it travels in space? This is a fun space activity for children that will challenge their design and building skills as well as their general knowledge of space.

- Put your design and building skills to the test by creating one of these objects using available resources such as various recycled household objects (including cardboard, tin foil, soft drink bottles, milk cartoons, newspaper, and more).

- Having a premade space station, spaceship, or satellite to the show the children is a good idea, as it will give them a rough guide to what is possible with their own designs.

Instructions

- Decide on what equipment you will use to make your space station, spaceship, or satellite.

- Choose which space object you would like to build and plan the design on paper before building.

- Start building! Try to follow your original design as much as possible, but it's okay to make changes.

- When you've finished, show off your finished creation to others and answer any questions they might have regarding your project.

Good questions include the following:

- Why did you choose to build this?

- What does this part do?

- Do astronauts live in your creation? If yes, where?

- What was the hardest part of building your space object?

- How well do you think you followed your original design? What would you do differently next time?

Was Christopher Columbus a heroic explorer or a villainous invader?

Can you solve this Mystery and answer the question *Was Christopher Columbus a heroic explorer or a villainous invader*? Explore (see what I did there?) the following cards to build an answer to this long-debated question. You may want to sort the information into sets to help you analyse and process it.

Possible sets could include the following:

- Explorer, invader, hero, villain

- Positive evidence, negative evidence, irrelevant (not helpful) evidence

- Good for Europe, bad for Europe, good for the Americas, bad for the Americas

You may also want to think about questions like these:

- Is some of the information more important or more weighted than other information?
- Are you judging him as a modern-day hero explorer / villainous invader or a 15th-century hero explorer / villainous invader? Is there a difference?
- Are you judging him from the perspective of the Native American people of the time or the European people of the time?

His parents were called Susanna and Domenico Columbus

©2020 www.challenginglearning.com

Columbus wanted to be a sailor when he was a young boy.

©2020 www.challenginglearning.com

During Columbus' time the only place to get riches such as silks and spices was to travel to the Indies

©2020 www.challenginglearning.com

Columbus met and married his wife Dona in Portugal.

©2020 www.challenginglearning.com

Aged 25 Columbus; ship was attacked by French pirates and sank off the coast of Portugal.

©2020 www.challenginglearning.com

Columbus wanted to sail west to try and reach the Indies as he thought this would be a quicker route.

©2020 www.challenginglearning.com

Europeans saw the discovery of the Americas as a chance to take lots of gold and riches for themselves.

©2020 www.challenginglearning.com

Columbus and his brother Bartholomew ran a shop in Portugal selling maps to strangers.

©2020 www.challenginglearning.com

Columbus was not the first European to set foot in the New World.

©2020 www.challenginglearning.com

Columbus and people at that time knew the earth was round but didn't know how big it was.

Christopher Columbus was born in Italy in 1451

Amerigo Vespucci charted the area and landed in the American continent around the same time as Columbus.

Columbus' discovery of the Americas led to many native cultures being wiped out or changed forever.

Columbus needed money to pay for his voyage west. The Kings of France and England refused to help.

The native people of the Americas had happily practiced their own tribal religions for many, many years before Columbus arrived.

When he arrived in the Americas, Columbus still thought he was in the Indies and called the local people Indians.

Columbus' journey to the Americas began 100's of years of exploration of the Americas

Columbus persevered for 10 years to secure funding for his voyage west.

Columbus' journey introduced corn, tomatoes and potatoes to European diets and wheat, coffee and sugar cane to the Americas.

His discovery of the Americas brought Columbus great fortune and positions of power.

Columbus died in 1506

When Columbus discovered the Americas he went back to Spain and told everyone about it.

The first land Columbus and his crew spotted on their journey was an island off the coast of Florida. They named it San Salvador.

Lief Eriksson led the Vikings to discover the Americas in the year 985.

The natives of Hispaniola were soon forced into slavery and punished with the loss of a limb or death if they did not collect enough gold for Columbus and his crew.

Columbus' voyages to the Americas enabled the exchange of plants, animals, cultures and ideas between the Old World and the New World.

Columbus was stripped of his title of Governor of the Spanish territories of Hispaniola by the Spanish King and Queen because of his mistreatment of the people there.

Challenging LEARNING   Lessons to support learning

The European sailors took many infectious diseases with them to the New World and many of the native people died within decades from these.

In 1492 the King and Queen of Spain gave him three ships and provisions to make the journey west.

When he was old enough Columbus became a sailor.

Columbus' son was called Diego.

The only known sail route to the Indies meant sailing east around Africa and was very long.

In August 1492 Columbus and his crew set sail in search of the Indies.

Columbus brought Christianity to groups of non-religious people.

Columbus' father was a weaver.

Columbus introduced technologies to the native people who were still largely hunters and gatherers.

At the age of 41 Columbus led four voyages across unknown and unchartered oceans in wooden sailing ships that were not designed to take on the rough Atlantic ocean.

Columbus travelled back to the Americas many time but still insisted he had found the Indies.

The Vikings did not tell anyone else about their discovery of the Americas.

Columbus agreed with the Spanish King and Queen that he could keep 10% of any gold, silver, spices, jewels or riches found.

Columbus created a very important bridge between the old world and the new world.

In October 1492 Columbus and his crew sighted land and thought they had reached the Indies.

The native people Columbus found on Hispaniola were unarmed and friendly. They were willing to trade goods with the sailors.

The European sailors treated the native people with cruel brutality.

Crossing the Atlantic ocean was a very rough and dangerous route and many sailors worried that they might fall off the edge of the Earth going that way.

Lessons to support learning

El Dorado and the exploration for gold

In 1848 gold was discovered in California. This led to what we now call the 'Gold Rush', as thousands of hopeful gold miners travelled over land and sea to explore the area to find gold for themselves. The county where the initial gold was found in California is now called 'El Dorado' after the legendary lost city of gold.

After Columbus arrived in the Americas, Europeans believed that exploration was the key to great wealth and riches. They thought there was a lost city of gold called El Dorado just waiting to be discovered, explored, and raided of its gold.

In the following poem, 'Eldorado' by Edgar Allan Poe, the poet refers to the shallow goal of exploring lands like California and El Dorado to take their treasure, to get rich, or to achieve fame. By comparing the Gold Rush with the search for Eldorado, he tells us that this kind of exploration does not bring us happiness; just as no one ever discovered the fabled city of gold, most of those exploring for gold in California did not get rich either.

Edgar Allan Poe tells us in this poem that the true value and riches of exploration are found in the experience of the journey you go on, not in whatever you find at the end. In the poem, Eldorado is the knight's goal, his dream, his destination – but he never even comes close to getting there. He's so focussed on the unrealistic Eldorado that he spends his whole life trying to find it, and in doing so, he misses all the sights along the way.

Poe is reminding us that we don't necessarily have to travel far and wide to enjoy the benefits of exploration.

Find the poem online or in a poetry book and read it out loud. Imagine with your child that you are the knight on a journey. This poem has a slow galloping rhythm, as if you are riding a horse. See if you can create a galloping rhythm by tapping it out.

Great writers are very careful and deliberate about the words they choose to use. Some of these words might be strange and unfamiliar to us. Here are a few:

Gaily bedight: dramatically dressed to look good

Gallant: brave and daring

Pilgrim: a traveller on a quest searching for something

Shade: a ghostly shadow

Allusions are references to well-known people, places, and things. 'Eldorado' is an allusion to a mythical place. See what you can find out about El Dorado. What was so great about it? Why would people risk their lives to find it?

Try writing your own poem about a journey of exploration. What is your goal? What are you hoping to discover? What might you see or experience on the journey? What interesting words could you use?

Exploration walks

Each day, go on a walk on the same route and follow the following directions (don't tell your child ahead of time what they will be doing each day). Take a notepad along and talk to your child about acting like a scientist, making observations as you go on your walks. If you have a clipboard to carry the notepad and a magnifying glass, it may create even more of a sense that your child is a scientist.

Day 1 – Look around and talk about and make notes about everything you notice.

Day 2 – Look for anything you see that is purple. Make notes or drawings of everything purple that you see.

Day 3 – Look for anything you see that is made out of metal. Make notes or drawings of everything metal that you see.

Day 4 – Look for anything you see that is moving. Make notes or drawings of everything you see that is moving.

Day 5 – Look for tall things. Keep track and make note of what the tallest things are that you see on your walk.

After all of your exploration walks, talk about the following:

- How were the walks different?
- Did you start to see things that you didn't even notice on your first walk?
- Did you notice any purple things, metal things, or moving things on the subsequent walks?
- What usually causes you to notice things when you are out walking?
- Why do you think there are some things that we don't usually notice or see?

The #selfie collage

Selfies are a way of allowing us to explore our self and our identity. One of the most effective ways to know yourself is to see yourself as others see you. Selfies offer opportunities to show different sides of yourself, such as the arty side, the silly side, the glamorous side, the serious side, or the adventurous side. Our understanding of others (and also of ourselves) is achieved by gathering together all the things we know about them. By looking at different sides of ourselves through images, we are sharing more of ourselves and making greater connections between the different aspects that make us the individuals we are.

Help your child to take (or draw) some selfies that

- clearly show their passions or interests,
- show the way they like to live life,
- reveal their likes and dislikes,
- reflect their social self,
- reflect their private self,
- share their personality.

Remember to make sure the selfies are normalising. It is not about creating the image of the 'perfect' you; you need to show the 'real' you. The 'perfect' or 'magazine image' does not exist, is usually not achievable, and is very superficial. It does not show all the wonderful, weird, and diverse qualities that make us who we are and make us interesting, loveable, and human.

Creating a self-exploration collage helps us to get to know ourselves in a different way. Images interact differently with the brain than words or text does. Images transfer experience. When we look at old photos, our brains relive the event along with the emotions of that experience.

Help your child use the selfies you have taken or drawn to create a self-exploration collage that they can use to really connect with and get to know themselves. Perhaps you can make one as well, and you and your child can talk about how well the pictures represent each of you.

Self-exploration inventory

To add to the collage(s), you can add a self-exploration inventory on the back of the collage. When you look at the collage later, you will not only be able to remember how your child (and you) looked, but also what they were interested in and cared about. Add details like the following:

- What kinds of dreams and goals for yourself do you have?
- Describe yourself in three words.
- What qualities do you most admire in yourself?
- What is one of your passions?
- In what ways are you like other members of your family or your friends?
- In what ways are you different to others?
- What is special about you?
- What do you most like to learn about?

Four corners – exploring, searching, invading, touring

Cut apart and read through the following cards with your child/ren. Talk about what is happening in each situation and what their reaction is to each one. Introduce the terms 'exploring', 'searching', 'invading', and 'touring'. Talk about what each one means and how the terms differ from one another.

Using the opinion corners frame that follows, encourage your child/ren to place the cards in the corner that they think best describes what is happening. They should place each quote in the correct corner on the opinion corners frame and give their reasons for their choices and their opinions about how they would describe each situation.

Challenge their reasons and thinking by asking questions like these:

- Why do you think that is searching rather than exploring?
- What is it about this one that makes you think that?
- If you say this is searching, can you explain how it is different from exploring?
- What would you change about the one you put in invading to make it either exploring or searching?

Going into a sibling's room, uninvited to look around.	Going into a sibling's room to look for a pen to borrow.	Going into a sibling's room to look for a pair of shoes that belong to you.	Looking for some of your sibling's candy in their room.
Taking a walk in the park and looking for wildlife, colorful flowers, or trees with different shaped leaves.	Walking through a park to look for a rock that you can turn into a pet rock.	Finding and keeping a toy that you find in a park.	Finding an island while on a boat ride and then walking around to see what is there.
Building a house and living on an island that you found while on a boat ride.	Walking around a resort to see what is there and what you can do.	Going into an "employee only" section of the resort to borrow a beach towel.	Walking along the beach at a resort looking for shells.

Opinion corners frame

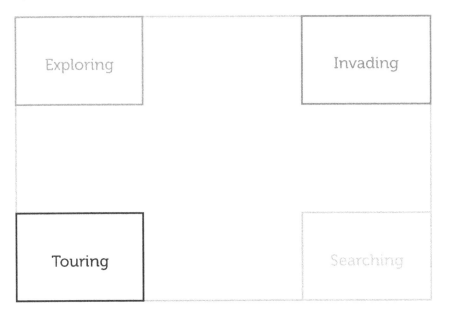

Concept target

Together with your child/ren, create a list of possible explorers and place them on a concept target. Write the examples that are most like explorers closer to the centre.

Here is a list to start you off using the concept target. If your child is able to come up with his/her own, don't use this list.

- Inventor
- Entrepreneur
- Scientist
- Author
- Historian
- Astronaut
- Musician
- Doctor

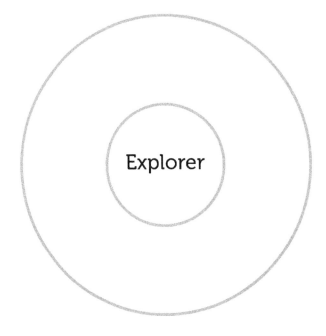

For this concept target, write the examples that best describe types of exploration closer to the centre.

- Tourism
- Dreaming
- Investigating
- Reading
- Researching
- Thinking
- Discussing
- Drawing

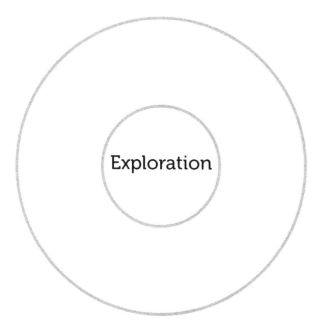

Number explorers

Tell your child that they are going to be a number explorer. Their job will be to explore all of the ways they can find to represent numbers. Talk first about different ways to show a particular number. Encourage your child to come up with ways such as addition or subtraction problems, tallies, coins representing the number as a value, words, objects representing the number, dice, dominoes, etc. Then challenge your children to come up with as many possible ways to represent numbers as they can. Have them first estimate how many ways they think they can find.

Give them a number and have them write/draw all of the ideas on paper, outside with chalk, on a whiteboard, etc.

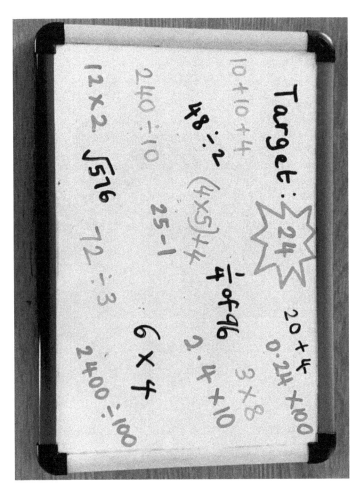

ChallengingLEARNING

Lessons to support learning

Why do we explore?

There are many reasons why people choose to explore. Some of these reasons are described on the cards that follow. Read through them with your child and then tell them that they will pretend to be the ruler of their country, and they must decide which types of exploration they will support. They must pick two that will be supported and funded by the country, two that will be allowed but at the expense of the explorer, and two that will be outlawed.

Talk about the following concepts:

What are the pros and cons of each?

Which of the reasons benefit more people?

Are there some reasons that are harmful to people or to the land?

Are there some reasons for exploring that have long-term benefits?

Trade	Treasures	Science
Many countries and rulers funded explorers in order to find new trade partners and goods. In some cases they hoped to find new trade routes that would help them to transport goods cheaper than their competitors. This was the case of Vasco da Gama and Christopher Columbus.	Often explorers have been in search of riches and treasure. The conquistadors were primarily searching for gold and silver when they conquered the Native Americans of the New World.	In many cases, explorers are scientists hoping to learn about nature and new parts of the world. They may be hoping to find a new species of animal or type of plant.

Recreation	Land	Challenge
Some explorers are just interested in the joy of the exploration. They want to see what is in the world around them, and they are interested in seeing a variety of places.	Many explorers claimed the land they found in the name of their country. Countries like Spain, Portugal, and Great Britain amassed huge empires during the Age of Exploration.	Many explorers want to test their personal limits and be the first in the world to do something. These types of explorers include the men who raced to be the first to the North and South Poles, to the top of Mount Everest, and to the moon.

Idea One:
If I don't stand up for myself, I will be considered weak

Idea Two:
It takes a lot of strength to turn your back and walk away from conflict

Dinner table conversations

Concept: Conflict

Main question: What is conflict?

Follow-up questions:

- What is the difference between conflict and disagreement?
- Does conflict always involve aggression or violence?
- How much is 'conflict' an everyday experience?
- How many different forms can conflict take?
- Is it impossible to go through life and never experience conflict?
- How much is 'conflict' a necessary part of progress?

Concept: Conflict

Main question: Is conflict a fact of life?

Follow-up questions:

- Is conflict unavoidable?
- Is it positive to have views and opinions that differ from others?
- Do you experience more conflict when you are older or younger?

- Can conflict be a creative process?
- Are all conflicts a negative experience?
- Can you be involved in conflict and not know it?
- What would life be like if conflict never existed?
- Is there such a thing as healthy conflict?

Concept: Conflict

Main question: Does conflict always start with disagreement?

Follow-up questions:
- What is the difference between dispute and conflict?
- Does conflict always involve confrontation?
- How often is conflict caused by a lack of respect for one another's needs and views?
- When might conflict be a necessary course of action?
- What role can conflict play in bringing about justice where injustice exists?
- What role do our beliefs and culture play in contributing to conflict?
- How might power and influence lead to conflict?

Concept: Conflict

Main question: What is the best way to respond to conflict?

Follow-up questions:
- Can all conflict be resolved?
- What is the importance of good communication in conflict resolution?
- How could a balance of power overcome potential conflict?
- Must one side be the victor over the other for conflict to be totally resolved?
- How important is peace building in the process of conflict resolution?
- Is conflict resolution always a positive thing?
- Does every conflict have a potential resolution, or can some never be resolved?

Game – conflicting Simon

Try this twist on the traditional Simon Says game to begin thinking about conflict as opposite.

- Like the traditional game, you will choose someone to be Simon, and everyone else will follow the directions given by Simon. For example, Simon will say, 'Simon says jump up and down', and everyone in the game will jump up and down.
- Simon continues to give directions, always starting with 'Simon says'.
- Here is the twist – when Simon gives a direction that does not start with 'Simon says', rather than NOT doing it, the players in the game have to do the OPPOSITE or something in conflict with it. For example, if Simon says 'stand up', everyone must sit down. Or if Simon says 'wave your hand', the players can wave a foot. Anyone who does not do an action that is opposite or at least conflicting with the action directed by Simon is out of the game.

Follow up with questions like these:

- What did you find challenging about this game? Was it more challenging to be Simon?
- What are some good directions for Simon to give that make it easy for the players to do the OPPOSITE?
- How can we change the game to make it MORE challenging?

Conflict and harmony

Battle	Clash	Competition	Struggle	War	Argument
Combat	Peace	Resolution	Agreement	Compromise	Surrender
Difference	Hatred	Disagreement	Similarity	Problem	Support

Encourage your child/ren to place the provided words on a line depending on how closely they are related to the word 'conflict' or not.

One end of the line should be labelled 'CONFLICT' and the other end labelled 'HARMONY'. Your child/ren need to decide whether the word is closer to the definition of harmony or the definition of conflict before they position it on the line. Each of the words needs to be considered in relation to the other words to decide their correct place on the line.

Questions to encourage thinking could include the following:

- Would 'battle' be closer to 'conflict' than 'war'? Why or why not?
- Where would 'compromise' be placed on the line?
- What is the difference between 'agreement' and 'resolution'?
- Which one these would you place closest to 'harmony'? Why?
- Which words are easy to position on the line?
- Which words are difficult to decide on where they should be placed?
- Can you add any words of your own?
- Are there any new words you have learned about 'conflict' and 'harmony'?

What is the difference between war and sport?

Over 3,000 years ago when sports came into existence, they involved preparation or training for war. Many early games involved the throwing of objects or sparring between opponents. During the first Olympic games in 776 BC, the Ancient Greeks brought formal sports into the world. Since that time, hundreds of new sports have evolved throughout the world. Many similarities, however, still exist between sport and war. Talk with your child about the similarities and differences, and generate a list of terms that are used with either sport or war. Use your list along with the words given here to compare and contrast sport and war. Challenge your child to come up with terms that ONLY apply to either war or sport.

Attack	Defend	Invade
Teams	Tactics	Challenge
Prevent	Block	Generals
Score	Armed forces	Leaders
Playing field	Compete	Win/Lose

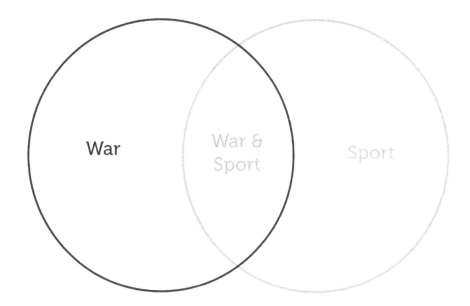

Challenge your child's thinking and reasoning as they make their choices.

- How is that term used in sport/war?
- Is that term used in the same way when discussing war as it is when discussing sport?
- How do we differentiate between sport and war?
- How do the goals differ between sport and war?

Ranking adaptations to nature conflicts

Talk to your child about what makes someone successful and what adaptations we have made to prepare for nature conflicts. Brainstorm some of the ways we have adapted our homes and buildings and ways that we prepare for conflicts with nature. Then cut out the following cards (and add any that you have come up with) and have your child arrange them into a diamond four (for younger children) or a diamond nine, placing the most important for protection and preparation at the top and the least important for protection and preparation at the bottom. Rearrange the cards as needed for each of the following (or come up with your own terms): earthquakes, tornadoes, hurricanes, flooding, fires, blizzards, ice storms, monsoons, tsunamis, avalanches/mudslides, volcanoes, thunderstorms, etc.

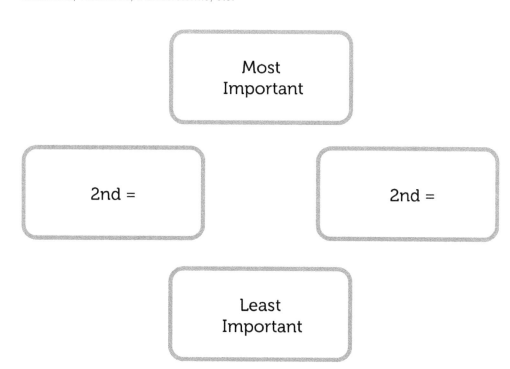

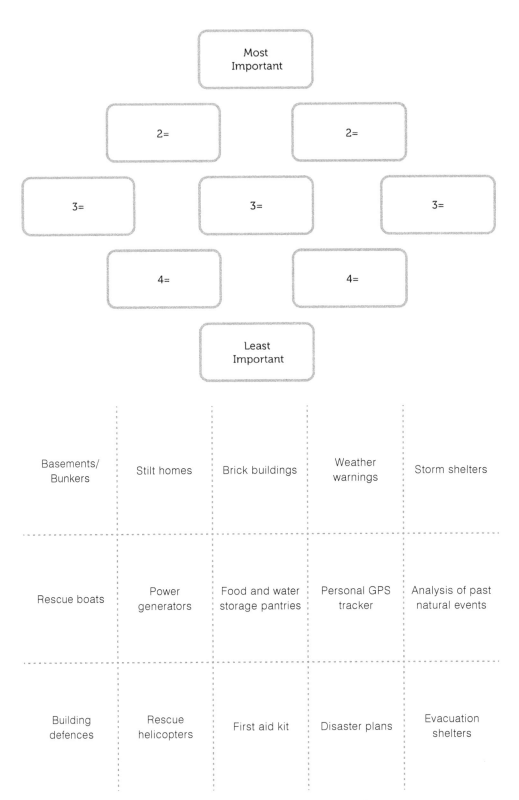

		Most Important		
	2=		2=	
3=		3=		3=
	4=		4=	
		Least Important		

Basements/ Bunkers	Stilt homes	Brick buildings	Weather warnings	Storm shelters
Rescue boats	Power generators	Food and water storage pantries	Personal GPS tracker	Analysis of past natural events
Building defences	Rescue helicopters	First aid kit	Disaster plans	Evacuation shelters

How did your rankings change with different nature conflicts?

Which adaptations were important in many of the conflicts? What makes them important?

How did you decide what was most important?

Conflict role-play

Sometimes two people are in conflict about something, and they have to work to come up with a compromise, a plan to share, or some other solution. Cut out the follow cards and put them into two groups, each with cards numbered 1–6 so that two people (you and your child, or two children) can role-play the conflicts. Start with one set of cards (both #1 cards). Each person reads the card to themselves before talking to one another to solve the conflict.

1

You and a friend
shovelled snow off of
a neighbour's driveway
together. You finished
after your friend had to
go home. You ended up
staying and hour and
your friend only stayed
for 45 minutes. The
neighbor paid $15.

1

You and a friend
shovelled snow off of
a neighbour's driveway
together. The neighbour
asked you to do it, but
you also invited your
friend. Your friend
didn't have any shovels,
so you used your
shovels.

2

You were assigned
a partner for a class
project. For the project
you have to build a solar
system model together.
You have swim practice
after school every day,
so you want to work on
it over the weekend.

2

You were assigned
a partner for a class
project. For the project
you have to build a solar
system model together.
You have a football
tournament over the
weekend, so you want
to work on it after
school.

3

You made a cup of chocolate milk and took it into the TV room. You realized you left your phone in your room, so you set the milk on a table while you ran up to your room. You came back to milk spilled on the sofa by your puppy.

3

You decided to let your new puppy out of her kennel to play. After letting her out, you went into the kitchen to grab a snack. You weren't watching the puppy and she went into the TV room. She knocked over a cup of milk.

4

Your boss asked you to indicate when you are available to work. You said you could work any weekday between 08:00 – 16:00 and you were scheduled from 08:00–12:00. You made plans with friends to go to the beach Friday at 13:00, but now you've been asked to work.

4

You ask your employees to provide available times to work each week and create work schedules based on their availability. You just found out that one of your employees has to leave early on Friday to attend a funeral, so you changed the schedule.

5

The night before your football game, you get all of your equipment together and put it in the car so that you are ready to go the next day. You are halfway to the game when you realize you are have taken the van and not the car.

5

Just before you are ready to leave for the football game, one of your children tells you he wants to go to a friend's house. You tell him to take the car because you are taking the van to the football game.

6

You go to a friend's house to play and the two of you build a fort by stacking books and toys and putting a sheet over them. While playing, you realize it is time for you to go home so you can join a group video game you had planned

6

A friend comes over to your house and you play in room after you had just cleaned it up. You take out all of your books and toys to make a fort and then your friend wants to go home.

Use the following prompts to start each conflict role-play discussion:

1 How do you think we should divide the money?
2 When should we work on the project?
3 Whose responsibility is it to clean up the milk?
4 Should someone be expected to work a time outside of their schedule?
5 How should we get the equipment to the game?
6 Whose job is it to clean up the room?

Static electricity – opposing forces

One definition of conflict is *a state of opposition between persons or ideas or interests*. In science, an example of opposition of forces is shown by one form of static electricity where two things with the same charge push each other away. You can set up the following experiment to demonstrate this.

Materials: two balloons and two pieces of yarn or string

Steps

1 Blow up both balloons and tie one piece of string to each balloon so that the balloons hang from the string.

2 Have your child rub one balloon on each side of their head.

3 Have your child hold the strings so that the balloons are hanging about 1 inch apart, but not touching. (The balloons should push each other away. If not, have your child rub the balloons on their hair again.)

4 Ask your child to draw/write their observations.

5 Have your child rub the balloon on their hair again and then pull the balloon about an inch from their hair.

6 Ask your child to draw/write their observations.

Follow-up questions: Start out by reminding your child that, with static electricity, two items with the same charge (both negative or both positive) push against one another, and two items with opposite charges (a positive and a negative) are attracted to one another.

- Why do you think the balloons pushed away from each other? Why is your hair pulled by the balloon?

- What do you think happens when you rub the balloon on your hair?

- How could we find out more about this?

- Can you think of other examples of static electricity?

- How might static electricity be a good thing? When could it be a problem?

- Can you think of other ways that we can show static electricity with the balloons? How can we change our experiment?

Conflicting numbers

It is likely that in your discussions about conflict, the concept of 'opposite' has surfaced. (Note: You may think this is a bit challenging for younger children, but even if they do not understand the concepts of addition and subtraction, they will likely understand the matching of red and black, which will help them in the future as they study integers.) Talk to your child about how, in maths, integers represent opposite numbers. Create a number line like the following to show the integers from −10 to +10.

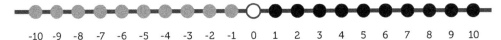

Talk about how the movement on the number line works – for example, when you move to the right, you are moving in a positive direction, and when you move to the left, you are moving in a negative direction. Use questions like the following, and use the terms 'positive' and 'negative' as much as possible:

- What is the difference between the numbers on the red side and the black side?

- Why do you think the numbers on the red side are arranged from largest to smallest and the numbers on the black side are arranged from smallest to largest?

- How can I describe the move from 4 to 6? How can I describe a move from 6 to 4?

- I have two pencils and then find three more. How can I use the number line to show the total number of pencils that I have?

- I found six flowers and gave three to my teacher. How can I use the number line to show the number of flowers that I now have?

Cut out 20 squares and colour ten of them black and ten of them red (or cut them out of black and red paper). Start out with just the ten black squares. Practice solving addition problems up to 10 using the squares AND the number line. For example, for 3 + 5, use the number line by starting on 3 and making five jumps, and use the squares by laying out three squares and five squares and then counting the total. Now use some of the following tasks/questions to help your child explore the negative numbers.

- *Write the problem 1 + −1.* How do you think we can show this problem on the number line? Using the squares? *Try it again with 2 + −2 and 3 + −3.* What do you notice is happening? *Help your child to see that a black square and a red square always make zero, so by pairing them, they can cancel each other out.*

- *Write the problem 5 + −6.* How can we show this problem using the number line? Using the squares?

- *Write the problem −4 + −3.* How can we show this problem using squares? How can we show this problem using the number line? How is this different than adding positive numbers?

For a challenge, introduce subtraction with integers using the following scaffolding questions. Do not go to the next question too soon. Let your child engage in the challenge by struggling and trying new things.

- *Write the problem 5 − (−3).* How can we solve this using the squares?

- If we start with five black squares, how can we subtract / take away three red squares?

- How can we use what we learned earlier – that one black square and one red square equal zero?

- What if I add a black square and a red square to the five black squares – have I changed the value?

- How can I add three red squares and still have a positive 5?

- Now can I take away three red squares? What is the answer to my problem?

Try additional problems while asking your child what they notice.

Conflict in literature (stories)

In literature or stories, conflict appears in the form of a struggle of some kind. Having conflict in a story gives it excitement and tension, and it makes it more interesting.

Types of story conflict

Character vs character	Character vs nature	Character vs themselves
• Heroes vs villains	• Severe weather problems	• Internal conflict
• Problems in romance	• End of the world	• Fighting personal desires
• Family dramas	• Struggles with animals or wildlife	• Struggles with fears
• Crimes against others	• Stranded on desert island	• Moral struggle
• Love rivals	• Shipwrecks	• Low self-worth or self-confidence
• Bullies		• Guilty conscience
• Friendship issues		

Character vs society	Character vs fate	Character vs technology
• Disobeying rules	• Fighting the future	• Science fiction
• Breaking the law	• Destiny	• Space travel
• Rebellions	• Gods	• Robots, androids
• Riots and protests	• Prophecies	• Machinery problems
• Feeling an outcast	• Premonitions	

Character vs supernatural	Add your own examples here:
• Monsters	
• Ghosts	
• Black magic	
• Vampires	
• Aliens	

Story conflict examples

Two characters are angry at each other	A character fights for survival in a storm	A character tries to defeat an evil ruling power
A character is being bullied by another character	A character is shipwrecked on a desert island	A character fights against their desire for revenge
A character rebels against the school system	A character feels lonely and like nobody understands them	A character battles to catch and kill a man-eating shark
A robot goes bad and turns against the family it lives with	A town is flooded after a major storm	A character tames some wild lions and keeps them as pets
A character is very jealous of others and struggles to control their anger	A character falls in love with their best friend's boyfriend	A character feels guilty about the accidental death of another character
A character stands up for another character who is being bullied because of the way they look	A mobile phone takes on a life of its own and starts causing trouble for its owner	A character is addicted to playing electronic games
A character changes the way the community thinks of them	A wicked witch tries to become a good witch	A character loses their memories and has to learn who they are all over again
A character is swallowed by a huge whale	A character tries to make a new life on another planet	A character thinks they are a duck but finds out they are actually a swan

Challenges

1   Match the story conflict examples to the type of story conflict you think they represent. Could some examples fit in more than one 'conflict type'?

2   Add some examples of your own to each 'conflict type'.

3   Do some research: look through storybooks you have, identify the conflict within a book, and determine what type of conflict it is. Some stories will have more than one example of conflict.

4   Take one of the 'conflict examples' and develop it into a story of your own.

Further examples of conflict types in young people's stories include the following:

Character vs character

- 'Rumpelstiltskin'
- *The Tale of Peter Rabbit*
- 'Snow White and the Seven Dwarves'
- *The Three Little Wolves and the Big Bad Pig*

Character vs nature

- *Moby Dick*
- *Charlotte's Web*
- *The Day the Crayons Quit*
- *The Jungle Book*
- *Lost and Found*

Character vs themselves

- 'The Boy Who Cried Wolf'
- *Owl Babies*
- *Koala Lou*
- *Where the Wild Things Are*
- *The Little Prince*

Character vs society

- *The Diary of Anne Frank*
- *The Hunger Games*
- *Wonder*
- *Holes*
- *The Lion, the Witch and the Wardrobe*

Character vs fate

- *Charlie and the Chocolate Factory*
- *Goodbye Mog*
- *Greyfriars Bobby*
- *My Henry*

Character vs technology

- *It's a Book*
- *The Iron Man*
- *#Goldilocks*
- *The Dot*

Character vs supernatural

- *Harry Potter* books
- *Artemis Fowl*
- *Inkheart*
- *Beegu*
- *The Gruffalo*

Add your own examples here:

NOTES

1   https://twitter.com/DrMayaAngelou/status/737308620186996736

2   www.forbes.com/sites/kevinkruse/2012/12/27/norman-schwarzkopf-quotes/?sh=7a9c9a194eeb

3   Interview published with the *Biograph* album set, 1985

4   www.notable-quotes.com/h/heroes_quotes.html

INDEX

CPSIA information can be obtained
at www.ICGtesting.com
Printed in the USA
LVHW060026210223
739952LV00007B/642

9 780367 772130